Bert,
I hope this adds
to your collection and you
enjoy the stories.
Chance
2/27/11

SOME MORE
HORSE
TRADIN'

BEN K. GREEN

SOME MORE HORSE TRADIN'

CASTLE BOOKS

This edition published in 2005 by
CASTLE BOOKS ®
A division of Book Sales, Inc.
114 Northfield Avenue
Edison, NJ 08837

This edition published by arrangement with and permission of
Alfred A. Knopf
A division of Random House, Inc.
1745 Broadway
New York, New York 10019

Originally published September 14, 1972

Library of Congress Cataloging-in-Publication Data:

Green, Ben K.
Some more horse tradin'.
1.   Horse buying. 2. Horses—Legends and stories. I. Title.

SF301.G744
636.1'08'1   70-38336

ISBN-13: 978-0-7858-2098-7
ISBN-10: 0-7858-2098-1

Printed in the United States of America

CONTENTS

Runaway!

3

*Mr. Undertaker and
the Cleveland Bay Horse*

23

Fast Mule Buyer

33

The Shield Mares

39

Watermelon Hauler's Mule

83

Gittin' Even

89

*Water Treatment
and the Sore-Tailed Bronc*

101

Cindy

111

Brethren Horse Traders

119

*Texas Cow Horses and
the Vermont Maid*

127

Mule Schoolin'

157

Saddle Marks

167

Fence Trouble

179

Foreign Trade

187

*The Last Trail Drive Through
Downtown Dallas*

197

SOME MORE
HORSE
TRADIN'

RUNAWAY!

I had been into deep South Texas with a string of tradin' horses and had sold out the last ones at Gonzales, Texas. I was ridin' a good, head-noddin', fox-trottin' light sorrel saddle horse with a flax mane and tail, about fifteen hands high, that wasn't good for a lot of things, but was a nice road horse that could drift you across the country with that natural swingin' fox trot, apparently with little effort on his part and little jar on the rider's part.

We had been several days coming back north when I rode into Waco and it was First Monday Trade's Day. The city of Waco is big, so I skirted around the edges and came in on the trade square not far from the Brazos River in the old part of town. It was early fall and there was lots of good horses and mules, milk cows, and other livestock on the square. There was already a little cotton money in circulation and traders and farmers alike were tryin' to have some business.

I had had a good trip and was carryin' plenty of tradin' money but wasn't too anxious to buy a bunch of common stock. I did think if there was something pretty nice in the way of saddle horses that would also do for light harness that I

might buy a choice one or two. Since I was mounted on a good horse, I wasn't too anxious to swap off, so I was more of a buyer than a trader, and anytime a trader is usin' fresh money to buy fresh stock he is harder to please than when he's tryin' to swap off something. So I spent the morning ridin' around among the tradin' stock exercisin' my hard critical eye.

A little after noon a nicely dressed middle-aged gentleman drove in on the square a fine-lookin' matched pair of dark brown geldings hooked to a buckboard that had been hand made out of several different kinds of wood and had been finished with a clear lacquer that brought out the natural grain of the oak, bois d'arc, cedar, and maybe some other kinds of wood I didn't recognize in this beautiful rig. The harness wasn't fancy nor dressed up with a lot of bright buckles and other hardware, but when you slipped your hands over the reins and along the tugs you were quickly impressed that it was all nice English tanned soft leather.

I had never seen a pair of horses like these. They were almost sixteen hands tall with a great deal of bone and substance and probably weighed thirteen or fourteen hundred pounds apiece. They didn't carry any heavy hair around the back of their legs or fetlocks and there was no coarseness about their joints, yet at the same time they were heavy horses that had the appearance of some of the light-boned breeds.

I tied my saddle horse to a hitchrack and jingled my spurs across to where this team stood. Fresh stock on the trade square always draws some lookers and some bright conversation. I felt like I was a little out of my class on this team and this nicely finished natural-grained wood rig, so I stood around and listened a good while. This was a well-mannered pair of big horses and I got a glimpse in their mouths when somebody else was lookin'. Their teeth were long and well shaped and showed to be younger by the table of the tooth than they actually were. This meant two things. They had good teeth to begin with and had been so well cared for and fed such good feed that their teeth had not been worn off what would be considered a normal amount for their years. Their legs were without blemish and they were deep-chested with a well-balanced topline. Their heads showed some refinement but still weren't small.

I studied this pair of horses and listened for about an hour and a half before I showed any interest in wanting to buy them. I finally asked this store-bought-lookin' gentleman that was drivin' the team what he would ask for them. He said that he would want to sell the team, the rig, and the harness and that he would take $500 and hand me the lines and I could figure the horses for whatever part of that $500 that I thought they were worth and the rig and the harness would be the difference.

I went back to my saddle horse and set in the shade of the tree by the hitchin' post and watched that beautiful team of drivin' horses. Their manners seemed to be the best and I noticed that there weren't any traders or any farmers could walk by them without givin' them the second look. I hadn't worried exactly about what use I had for this team and rig or about what I would do with them after I bought 'em, but that quality would knock a country boy's eyes out and I knew I could own 'em for a little while even if I had to sell 'em later on.

I was almost a stranger in a strange land and I didn't see anybody I knew to ask about the team. Late in the afternoon, I made a bid of $425 that seemed to insult this town-bred gentleman, but along towards sundown he hadn't had any better offers and I watched him work himself around through the horses and mules and visit a little bit as he got over close to where I had been loafin' with my horse. It seemed to me it would be a good time to break him down a little, so I got on my horse and started to ride off. Just as I expected, he hollered at me to wait a minute.

He told me I was lettin' $75 cheat me out of the best

driving team that had ever lived and the most beautiful
buckboard. I said I wouldn't let $75 do that to me and he
was quotin' it wrong—that he was lettin' $75 cheat him out
of $425. Well, that kind of intellectual figurin' went on until
he finally offered to take $450. I told him that I didn't be-
lieve I wanted to raise my bid, and it had begun to run
through my mind that I hadn't seen these horses work except when he drove them in on the square and I said, "Before
I would give $450 for them, I believe I would want to drive
'em."

He said, "Well, let's go over and have another look."

As he put in a little light conversation, he said, "I believe
I'm just goin' to go ahead and trade with you and take the
$425."

Well, he didn't know it, but I was sweatin' worse than he
was and was goin' to give the $25 extra so to cinch the deal
right quick, so I counted out the money. I put a lariat rope
around my saddle horse's neck and tied it where it wouldn't
choke him. After I took his bridle off and tied it to the saddle
horn, I stepped up into the rig and took a hold of my new
drivin' team and let my saddle horse trot along on a loose
rope since I hadn't tied it anywhere to the buckboard; I had
it draped over the spring seat next to where I was.

As I left town, I went across the Brazos River and drove
over to East Terrace, which was a few acres of land with a
great big old-timey two-story brick house on it that belonged
to Howard Mann. Howard was a fine old-time horseman
whom time, and I guess progress, had overtaken. Most of this
world's goods had slipped through his fingers, but he still
had good judgment and expensive tastes. As I drove up to
circle around in the front, Howard came off the porch,
showin' a big burst of enthusiasm for an old man. I hadn't
seen him for a year or so, and of course we shook hands. I
got down on the ground and we had just started to visit
when Howard looked at the rig and the team and said, "I'm
glad you have gotten Dr. Bond's team of Heidelberg harness

horses. They're the finest driving horses that have ever been in Waco." And as he laughed he said, "Probably the meanest, but that won't bother you any."

I asked, "Why do you say they're the meanest, Howard?"

He said, "Oh Ben, they're not really mean, they're just bad to run away. You see those two front wheels that have been built out of bois d'arc and so beautifully lacquered. Well, they used to be oak like the two back wheels, but during runaways these horses ruined both wheels and Dr. Bond had Old Man Shultz build replacements out of bois d'arc, thinking maybe they would be harder to break up."

And he said, "All these extra pieces of cedar you see in this bed is where they have replaced boards after different runaways. That buckboard originally had a stationary spring seat and it was broken off so many times that finally Old Man Shultz put a portable spring seat on that rig just like you would find on a wagon."

As he told me all this, he kept tellin' me, "Ben, this won't bother you. You aren't afraid of a runaway team and you'll figure out a way to break them." And as an afterthought he said, "I just imagine a few days' work to a loaded wagon might stop a lot of that."

I didn't stay too long with Howard and turned up the road north toward Hillsboro. I thought I would drive until about dark or till I found a good campin' place. These nice big horses moved along in a fair trot—not so fast but what my saddle horse could keep up without strikin' a lope—and we got along fine drivin' up the side of the road out of the traffic.

About dark, I pulled out by the side of the road at Elm Mott under some big trees and made camp for the night. I had picked up some feed as I left Waco, so I let my saddle horse eat off the back of the buckboard and tied my drivin' team to a big gentle tree and poured their feed on the ground where they could eat together.

Next morning I hooked up and threw my saddle on the

buckboard and thought I would I would tie my saddle horse. Then I got to thinkin' about that runaway team so I ran my lariat rope all the way up to my spring seat and tied it in a slipknot around one of the springs where I could reach down and jerk it loose in case I needed to. I had been driving this good team up the road at just a brisk trot and after about five miles of warming up had let them break into a good moving kind of road trot that would get you over lots of country in a day.

We crossed a concrete bridge with banisters and just as I cleared the north end, these horses suddenly found them a spook and broke to run away. When I took hold of the lines to try to check them, they had both cold-jawed and clamped their bits between their teeth. With their size, arched necks, and stout bodies, it would have been a joke for me to have thought I could hold them. I reached back and jerked the slipknot to untie my saddle horse to keep from draggin' him.

About half a mile in front of me I saw a country road curving off at an angle to the right. I dropped what pull I had on the left line and pulled on the right line just enough to throw their balance to where they would go up that country road. When I knew I had them on that country road and there wasn't anybody comin', I reached and got a bull whip that had been tied on my saddle and started knockin' hair off those big horses about every time they hit the ground and furnishin' them all the slack that I could on the line. It came as a sudden shock to them that there wasn't goin' to be any screamin' and pullin' and tryin' to keep them from runnin' and when it looked like they were goin' to show some sense and slow down, I laid the leather on them and hollered some more. I went through the little town of Leroy and I still had up speed. When I was almost in view of Mt. Calm and the road was even less populated, this ball of fast horses began to lose interest in tryin' to leave this earth.

I had been squattin' down behind the seat on my knees just in case somethin' might happen, because I didn't want to get thrown over on the team, and I knew better than to stand up, because I might get thrown out on either side. I was a little tired of this, so I stepped over the spring seat and set down. By now this pair of big stout horses were wringin' wet with sweat, and lather was workin' out from under their harness. I didn't think that I wanted to windbreak them, but I didn't want them to think it was goin' to be a short day so I spoke to them without takin' the slack out of my lines and they slowed up to a lope.

There was a big wide place where the road forked and I dropped the slack on the right line and shook the left line before I pulled on it, and, sure enough, they had turned the bits loose, so I drew them down and turned them around. This had been a seven- or eight-mile run and as we turned around they dropped down into a slow trot. I didn't squall at them or pull on them and in another mile they had slowed down to just a good average walk and were tryin' hard to get enough breath to live on since they were pretty well winded. In about an hour and a half I got back to the road where I had turned my saddle horse loose and he was very comfortably grazin' along the right of way and draggin' his lead rope.

This time I thought that it might be smart to tie him up even with the team, so I tied him to the right hand horse's harness on a fairly short rope to where if we had another horse race, he could be in it and I wouln't have to come back after him.

By now these horses were cooled out good and had very little live sweat on them, so I clucked to 'em and popped the lines over their backs and struck a pretty good travelin' sort of trot and we got into Hillsboro in about middle of the afternoon. I went to the wagonyard to put up my horses and loaf around awhile before dark.

Next morning I took a lot of time to brush and curry the dried sweat off this drivin' team that thought they were racehorses and to wipe their nostrils and eyes out with a damp sack and clean out and clean off their feet and give them the attention they had been used to. I took the harness to the water trough and dipped it in and then wiped the dirt and sweat off with my hands before I harnessed the team and hooked them to the buckboard.

The usual kind of horse and mule dealers were standin' around that morning as I was gettin' ready to leave and they, of course, tried me on price with no intentions of buyin'. I knew they were just wonderin' what a team like that was worth, so I priced the team and rig for $750. I didn't get much back talk because, for the most part, none of them knew whether the deal was high or cheap.

This pair of nice big horses hadn't been used very much lately, probably because of their bad habits, and they were sore and stiff from the runaway that they had pulled and the day's work that I put on 'em along with it, but I had my doubts about them stayin' stiff too long, so I tied my saddle horse to the hame of the right-hand horse. We hit a slow jog trot in the edge of Hillsboro headed north. These big horses warmed up and seemed like they were goin' to drive real nice.

I stopped up about middle of the morning at Itasca and drove around behind the stores and tied my team to a hitch-rack. I don't know exactly what caused me to think to do it, but I untied my saddle horse from the hame and tied him to the hitchrack by himself. I hadn't tied this team before and I just used the nice light leather straps that snapped on to the bits and tied each horse to the hitchrack.

I was just goin' to walk around town and loaf a little bit and went into the grocery store to buy some grub to eat later on in the day. I had paid for my groceries and had the sack in my arm when I heard two or three people holler, "There goes a runaway team!"

The grocery store was on the corner of the street and I stepped to the door and watched them pass. I was real glad I had a saddle horse tied separate. I put the rope around his nose and jumped on him bareback and broke off in a lope acarryin' that sack of groceries in one arm and the coiled up end of the rope in the other, and between nursin' that sack of groceries and ridin' that horse with a rope on his nose, I wasn't in too good a shape to catch a runaway team. However, I thought that if I couldn't keep up, I would catch up when something happened to 'em.

They were about a mile out of town on a country road runnin' about full tilt and apoppin' that buckboard back and forth behind them when a farmer drivin' a team of mules to a wagon with a cultivator hooked on behind the wagon drove across the road in front of them before he saw them comin' and could get out of the way. This pair of runaways wasn't too badly scared. They were just runnin' for fun because they swerved over by the side of the road and stopped by themselves to keep from runnin' into the barbwire fence and went to grazin'. I was just a little piece behind and I was mad enough to kill 'em, but, at the same time, I was awful glad that they hadn't tore up my rig.

I pulled my saddle horse up to a walk and reined him to the far side of the road and went past them like I didn't know they were there. Then I slipped off my horse and walked back facing them and got a hold of their lines. They had their mouths full of grass and were actin' as innocent as horses can act with broken tie straps hangin' from each pair of bits. I had found out something else about 'em. They would break tie straps to get to run away.

I kept a pretty tight line on 'em the rest of the day and drove into Alvarado and found an old man with a good barn and plenty of feed that would let me put my team up overnight. I had my saddle blanket and a blanket tied on the back of my saddle so I made a pallet in the back of the buckboard and spent the night.

Next morning I got to thinkin' that if I sat up straight and popped a whip over that team I could drive to Weatherford by dark. It would be hard on my saddle horse to have to travel alongside of them, but I didn't think it would hurt that big team of Heidelberg coach horses. So far as I was concerned, the hard-headed German was stickin' out in 'em worse every day.

I stopped on market square at Cleburne to water my horses. There was a country café right by the trade ground. I hollered at the cook to make me some hamburgers to take with me and bring them out to me and I didn't leave my team.

The road from Cleburne to Weatherford was a gravel sur-faced road with not too much traffic, and I felt like if I just kept 'em at a steady trot that I might take some of that run out of 'em. I drove into Godley in a couple of hours and had these old ponies wet with sweat and breathin' a little hard and I felt like I was doin' 'em a whole lot of good. About the time I got even with the schoolhouse, the band was out on the grounds and decided to practice, and on the first big blow these kids gave on their horns, the runaway was on. The trip up to now hadn't hurt 'em, and I just thought they was breathin' hard!

I managed to hold 'em in the road and I sawed on the bits and in about three miles discouraged them down to a trot. When I finally got them to where they would turn loose the bits and would stop, I unwired a piece of balin' wire that was hangin' to the buckboard and held on to the lines and walked to the front of 'em. I took the bits out of each horse's mouth and wrapped them good with that balin' wire, which is a pretty brutal thing on a horse's mouth, but these horses weren't causin' me to develop too much affection for them, and I felt like if I made it more brutal on their mouths, it might be easier on my arms to hold them.

In just a little while they became real sensitive to that wire on their bits and I thought maybe this would be the little trick that would keep their minds on their business. It was gettin' late in the afternoon when I drove through Cresson and I really thought that I might stop somewhere and spend the night. The railroad track ran parallel to the road, and about the time I was havin' some of these kind-hearted thoughts, a train whistle blew and I thought, here's where I tear their mouths open with that wire, but they had had time to learn about that wire and they took those bits beween their jaw teeth and cold-jawed and I couldn't move that wire to make them a little remorseful by tearin' some hide off their mouths.

I didn't see nobody comin' and nobody behind me and no way for anybody to help and this was the second time they had run away that day. The one thing that was botherin' me was that I was feelin' sorry for my saddle horse havin' to keep up with 'em. After all, he hadn't done anything wrong. And it so happened that he was thinkin' the same thing I was and decided he had had enough of that foolishness, so he reared back on that good stout rope tied to that right-hand horse's hame. He caught that big horse in the air and jerked him and the other horse sideways and drug 'em just a step or two, and in the scuffle the right-hand horse that the saddle horse was tied to fell to the ground sideways and the left-hand horse stopped just a second after they had broke the tongue out of the buckboard. I eased out of the buckboard, thinkin' how lucky I was that it didn't turn over As this one horse got up, I spanked my saddle horse with my line just enough to make him straighten up and I drove them over to the fence still hooked to the tongue.

I cut the long end of the rope that my saddle horse was tied with and tied one end around one horse's neck and down through his bits and over to the other horse's bits and then around his neck and then to a big heavy cedar fencepost. I stood and looked at 'em and kind of got over the shock of the runaway and then I very carefully unhooked them from the tongue they were draggin' and carried it back to the buckboard so I could try to figure out how to patch it enough to get home.

It was broken where the doubletree hooks onto the tongue.

About all the tongue does is to furnish a way to guide the buckboard, so I wired the doubletree to the part of the tongue that was still hooked to the buckboard behind the break in the tongue. Then I took some barbwire off the fence by the road and wired the tongue back together and ran the barbwire back to the axle and wrapped it around the tongue and up to the front of the tongue and then I wrapped it around the breast yoke and tied it back against the front end of the tongue. This made a pretty crude kind of a front end, but I thought it would guide well enough that I could drive it home.

By now it was nearly dark and I rehooked my runaway team with my saddle horse tied to 'em and started up the road. I guess they had intended this last little spree to pay off better—they figured they'd get turned loose—and they seemed to wilt a little bit when I hooked them back up. I don't know whether or not they savvied what a weak tongue they were hooked to, but the doubletree was wired hard and fast and they had a firm pull on the rig. It was about midnight when I drove in home. It had been about a forty-five-mile day and these old ponies seemed give out and appeared to be so gentle that I thought they never would run again.

The next morning I got Guy Oliver at the blacksmith shop to repair the tongue with some iron straps, makin' it hell for stout. Since I had been gone a couple of weeks or more, I had some ridin' to do to tend to my livestock, some errands to run, and things to see about, so it was several days before I hooked up my fancy pair of drivin' horses. It was a bright Saturday afternoon and there were lots of people in town and I thought it would be a good time to show off my drivin' team and rig. I don't suppose I thought anybody would be interested in buyin' them. I just wanted to show off.

I drove up and down the street and around the square down to the wagonyard and these fine horses had so much style and moved so gracefully that old horsemen would stop on the sidewalk and turn and watch them pass. I could see our reflection in the plate-glass windows in the stores and I sure sat up straight and held a tight line and let everybody get an eyeful.

I drove down to the wagonyard and tied them in a spot where they couldn't very well break loose or get away, and I had no sooner tied 'em than twenty-five or thirty people gathered around 'em. Some followed 'em from uptown and there was lots of conversation about what a fine team they were. Many people didn't realize what their breeding was until I would tell 'em. I didn't offer to untie 'em and take anybody drivin' because I thought that would be just the right inspiration for that pair to have a runaway.

In the late afternoon I started out South Main toward home and a bunch of college kids were practicin' basketball. The ball bounced out in the middle of the road with two or three of them players wearin' colored uniforms after it, and just before the team thought to run away, I jerked those balin'-wire bits through their mouths before they could take the cold jaw and drove 'em on home with nobody knowin' that they almost saw a runaway.

I didn't keep my secret very long because I took a bunch of kids on a hayride one night and that pair of big fine trottin' horses ran away going up Oyster Hill and rolled school kids from the top of the hill to the bottom. I managed to swerve 'em into a live-oak thicket and get their heads and harness tangled up to where they wouldn't hurt themselves nor my rig. We was gonna have a wiener roast, so the kids gathered up on Oyster Hill and built a fire. We had our wiener roast and forgot about the danger of ridin' in that buckboard and crawled back in it. Oyster Hill was steep which ever way you went up or down it and them squallin' kids hollerin' and laughin' and the load pushin' down on the britchin' harness made this pair awful nervous, but while I had 'em up in that live-oak thicket I ran a big heavy rope across from one back wheel to the other back wheel and tied it hard and fast. Then when we moved, this rope worked up to and stopped the wheels when it came in contact with the buckboard bed. This made the team have to pull real hard with those wheels slidin'. I managed to get everybody delivered home safe and got back to the barn with two wheels still draggin'.

Well, by morning the kids had told all their folks about the runaway team. Some of them thought it was pretty funny, but some of the old women took it pretty serious and gave me a good talkin' to about being careless with their little children. They didn't seem to bother about me.

By now I had begun to develop some scare for this old pair of ponies and had took to drivin' em in a big oat stubble field as I tried different ways to keep them from runnin' away and methods to stop them. I used a walking W, smotherin' straps on their bridles, and about anything else I could think of or heard somebody else suggest. Nothing phased this determined pair of fast-minded horses.

They spent about two or three months around the barn without too much work and I was pretty sick of the deal and could think of a lot of things that I wished I had spent that money on instead of that pair of Kaiser-bred horses. I was takin' a good deal of hurrahin' from the traders around town about not drivin' my "Sunday rig," as they referred to it.

Pretty soon in the early fall, the town was plastered with them big loud signs and billboards and circulars of various sizes with all kinds of pictures on 'em that Ringling Bros. and Barnum and Bailey Circus was comin' to town. Of course, they would unload at the railroad with their teams and have a big parade through town to the circus grounds at the end of South Main. I thought that this would be a good place to show off my team and either scare 'em to death with the big animals or have a runaway and lead the parade.

The afternoon before the circus was comin' I brushed and curried and cleaned them off real good and washed the wheels and the bed of the buckboard, and the next morning about daylight I got them to the railroad station, where all the commotion was. I sat in the buckboard and watched the circus unload, but never let any slack come in the lines and never thought of leaving the team. This pair of big fine horses was scared to death all morning about something or other and the smell of them wild animals got their minds off of runnin' away. There was so much goin' on that they didn't know anything to do but stand and snort and stomp and try to behave, hopin' nothin' bad would happen to 'em.

Every now and then somebody in the morning's crowd would notice my fine team and the teamsters that were unloadin' the circus wagons would stop and admire them. Strangers asked what the team was worth and they didn't realize I had some very positive opinions about what they were worth, but what I would take for them wasn't the same figure, and I would just say $1,000, which sounded like an awful lot of money, so the word was around in a little while among the circus people that I wanted $1,000 for that team.

I waited until the parade toward the show grounds got out in front of me and then I brought up the rear. I didn't believe this pair of bluffers would have the nerve to run away if they were goin' to have to pass a bunch of elephants and camels. They traveled up on the bits with their necks bowed and eyes open and snortin' all the way, and they was touchin' the ground so lightly that you wouldn't have thought their hooves would have made a print.

I was kinda enjoyin' havin' them mixed up in a bunch of company that they didn't know what to do with, so I stayed on the circus grounds with 'em all morning. They had the main tent up by dinner, and by now the show-horse trainer had found my team. He came and looked at them and walked around them. He was some kind of a foreigner and I couldn't quite understand him. He went off and brought back an old dressed-up man with long white hair and diamonds all over him, wearin' a double-breasted blue serge suit, a big white hat, and carryin' a walking cane. They looked at my horses and asked if they would drive in that tent—that they needed a team to lead the opening act that would travel like they was about to run away.

Well, I wanted to show plenty of nerve, so I invited them to get in the buckboard with me. The old dressed-up man got in the seat with me and lit a fresh cigar and the horse trainer stood up behind the seat as I drove in under the tent. I told them to drop the flaps of the tent door down where the horses couldn't see daylight, since they might try to leave.

It was a great big long show tent and you could get up a lot of speed before you would have to make a turn at the ends. As I brought them out of the first turn. the old gentleman was all smiles and had bit down on that cigar and said, "Son, turn them on!"

Most of the time I had been holding these horses instead of driving them and this was a new experience to have me squall at 'em. We made about the third round and had up lots of speed. I had took hold of the lines pretty hard and realized that they had cold-jawed and we was havin' a runaway and nobody but me and them knew it. The old man hollered in my ear, "They're just what we need. Stop 'em when we come around again."

He didn't know it, but I thought we might go around a lot of times before we got them stopped, but about that time somebody led a camel in the tent flap just as we were comin' down that side of the tent. I felt the lines give and saw slack come in the tugs all at the same time just as the team smelled that camel. I thought this was my chance and I hollered, "Whoa," real loud and they had loosened the bits enough that I jerked that balin' wire through their tender mouths and they slid to a stop. I had to reach over and hold the old man to keep him from sliding out on the floor. He straightened up and as he stepped out on the ground, he said, "I understand that you want $1,000 for the whole outfit."

I said, "Yes, sir, that's my price."

He turned to the horse trainer with a big smile on his face

and said, "Scotty, take them back to the horse tent," and he put his arm around my shoulders and said, "Let's go to the office wagon and I'll give you the money."

As he counted out $1,000 in big bills, I wanted awful bad to tell him to keep that camel in the act, but then I decided they would find that out later anyway.

MR. UNDERTAKER

AND THE

CLEVELAND

BAY

HORSE

About the time in my life that I had decided to my own satisfaction that I was bound to be the best cowboy, the best bronc rider, and the best all-round stockhand in the world (this kind of personal opinion generally develops in a cowboy about nineteen years old), I was ranchin' on Robinson Creek running a bunch of steers that were doin' real good. It had been a mild winter, an early spring, and now we were in the middle of a lush summer and I didn't have a whole lot to do at the ranch, so I was spending most of my time ridin' my best saddle horses back and forth to town to spend my leisure time.

We had a very upstanding businessman in the community that was in the furniture and undertaking business, and I hadn't developed too much taste for undertakers by this time in life. A wild, rough, young cowboy don't worry a whole lot about dying, and I failed to feel the need for the friendship of the local undertaker, so me and him wasn't on too brotherly terms. The only thing that interested me about this prominent citizen was a good blood bay horse that he used to drive to a delivery hack.

Autos had begun to infest the country pretty bad, but few people had anything that resembled a truck. Small-town businessmen still had delivery hacks that they drove one horse to or spring wagons that they usually drove small pony teams to that traveled easily in a trot.

Mr. Undertaker was one of those good charitable kind of people that would take a widow woman's cookstove on account to help pay for her husband's funeral. To say the least, I didn't consider him one of God's most noble chillun.

It caused me some unrest to see that good fat blood bay horse standing around in his lot, with so little to do, and then to be used in the kind of business that Mr. Undertaker put him to was not helping him any. I had heard rumors that this good horse wasn't too content with his station in life, pulling that little hack with secondhand furniture and such on it. Recently he had run away three times in one week, and Mr. Undertaker had developed some fear, either of his horse or the thought of being one of his own customers.

I had just rode by the little pasture beside the road and saw this good horse grazin' and thought, "What a waste of good horseflesh for that horse to be grazin' and standin' under the shade of a tree instead of being a mount for a cowboy."

I had tied my saddle mare to the chain around the courthouse square where everybody tied their horses, and had walked across the square to the drugstore. Mr. Undertaker happened to be coming out of the drugstore when he glanced up and saw me. Instead of looking off in the other direction, he smiled and stuck out his hand to shake hands with me.

He bragged on me a few minutes and told me what a fine horseman I was and if he had his life to do over, he'd try to make just as good a cowboy as everybody said that I'd made. Most people would have thanked him for that speech, but it put me on my guard. I said that I'd heard he had done very well at the business of waitin' around for his friends to die. You could tell he didn't think that remark was too funny, but he tried to force a smile that turned into a weak kind of grin. Since we had passed the pleasantries of the day, he said, "I think you should have my bay horse . . . to use as a saddle horse. He's a fine horse, a six-year-old, and sound in every way. I have so little use for him that he has become too 'spirited' for me to use here in town to my conveyance."

I said, "Yep, I done heard that he had run away a couple of times and splintered up one of them cane-bottom chairs that you probably took away from somebody and left settin' on the porch." He still didn't think that was funny, but there wasn't goin' to be no way of insultin' him when he had the business of lettin' me have that bad horse on his mind.

He started out again by sayin', "Everybody knows that that horse can't run away with YOU, so what do you have that you would trade me for him that I would be proud to have hooked to my delivery hack?"

I started out by sayin' that I didn't have no sorry horses and I'd just about soon trade him one as another, but since he had brought it up, the mare that was standin' there hitched to the chain around the courthouse was eight years old and was a standard-bred harness mare, and I'd guarantee her not to run away.

We walked out and looked at the mare; she was gentle to ride and was about the same color as his horse. He tried to conceal his anxiousness to trade for this mare by tellin' me that a mare wasn't worth as much as a horse and that he felt he wouldn't be able to trade even since there was a little difference in our horses' ages. I was quick to explain to him that two years difference in age might be one of the ways to account for the difference in her gentle disposition and his runaway horse. I let down pretty hard on that "runaway" when I said it, and you could see him flinch a little; but I knew his horse was worth about three times as much as my mare and I was hopin' he didn't know it too.

We talked on about as long as I wanted to be seen in his company on the public square. People might go to thinkin' that I was tryin' to be a friend of his and that wasn't too pleasant a thought so far as I was concerned. So I told him I wouldn't be interested in givin' any boot just to get a runaway horse, and started back toward the drugstore. He didn't move; he was standin' there lookin' at my mare, but I didn't glance back at him. I made him turn and call me by name to get me to stop. I knew then he was aweakenin' fast. It didn't take much more conversation till we had a horse trade.

His little pasture ran up to the back of the furniture store, and he said, "Just wait here with the mare and I'll go get the horse and lead him out there in front."

He thought he was real smart, but I was already wise to what was about to happen. When he brought his horse up, I unsaddled my mare and saddled this good bay horse that I had had a hankerin' for ever since the first time I saw him. He had good clean straight legs, a short back, a long slopin'

shoulder, and a beautiful head and neck. His breeding was
something different from the average stock of horses in the
country, but I really didn't know at the time what his an-
cestry might be.

I slipped the bridle off the mare and he put his lead rope
around her neck and then I put my bridle on the horse and
fastened the throat latch a little tight. This handsome horse
wasn't bein' mean, but he was showin' a lot of interest in
things. I led him around in a little circle a few minutes. I
reached up and took ahold of the cheek of the bridle with one
hand, twisted my stirrup, and reached for the saddle horn
and stepped on him and turned his head aloose.

He stood there for a few minutes and I could feel him
swellin' up under me and he'd begun to let his ears back. I
knew that he was fixin' to come undone! This didn't bother
me much because when he started the ruckus I was goin' to
help him. I was wearin' spoke rowel spurs and carryin' a
loaded quirt. I glanced around the little country town; business had stopped and everybody was out on the courthouse
square or standin' in the doorways awaitin' for a bronc ride.
Mr. Undertaker had a pretty good crowd listenin' and said
in his loudest tone of voice, "Ben, you forgot to ask me if he
was broke to ride!"

People began to laugh and holler up and down the street
and were waitin' for the show. I thought I could ride this
ole pony, but it seemed he had more reputation than I had
heard about or all the natives wouldn't be showin' so much
interest.

I pulled my hat down real tight and I felt my heels
quiverin' a little in my stirrups, and I decided I'd better hit
him before I got scared. I squalled at him and cut him across
the rump with that quirt; he jumped high enough the first
jump for me to scare the courthouse pigeons! When he hit
the ground, he bawled like a bull buffalo that had just been
caught on the cow catcher of an early-day train engine.

For the next few minutes I was awful busy . . . his head

made three in front and his tail made three behind . . . the place on his back where I cinched my saddle wasn't no bigger'n a prairie dog mound on a mountain. He bucked all the stuff out of my britches pockets—my pocketknife and change . . . and if my shirt hadn't been buttoned good, it would've come off me while we was sailin' on one of them long jumps through the air. I'd lost my hat, tore my finger-nails off on the saddle horn, and was damn near throwed when he lost his breath and throwed his head up and stopped!

This country courthouse square was graveled and the thought of being throwed on that hard ground had sure encouraged me to stay on, but if he'd made just one more jump, he would've had the battle won. The crowd was ahol-lerin' and agoin' wild, and you could still hear Mr. Under-taker when he could get his breath from laughin', being sure to tell all the natives that I hadn't asked if the horse was broken to ride.

Lester Lewis came out to the horse and eased up real careful and picked up the bridle reins and handed 'em back to me . . . you see, I lost them in the early part of the war. Lester was an old-time friend who was kind of a wore-out horse trader and mule dealer, and hadn't been in on this "What was goin' on" until he heard the commotion and had walked up the street from the livery stable.

He had gathered up my belongin's and my hat, and as he handed my stuff to me, he said in a low tone, "Ben, this horse has throwed a lot of good riders; don't you get off of him this side of bedtime."

I said, "Much obliged," and this time I wrapped the reins around my hand good and tight and pulled that old horse's head up way high where he couldn't buck and started out at the corner of the square headed to the northwest. Lipan was a good twenty miles away.

Of course, this horse was bridle-wise because he had been worked in harness. About five miles out of town he'd begun to walk pretty near like a common horse and my arms were gettin' tired so I let him have a little slack. When I passed through Thorp Springs I'd eased him up into a pretty good trot.

This episode started a little after dinner and I rode into Lipan about two hours after dark.

I had an old friend by the name of Ross that lived on the edge of town so I rode up to the edge of the yard and hollered, "Hello," which was the custom of the country when you rode into a man's house at night. Ross stuck his head out the door and hollered, "Git down!"

I said, "Hell, I don't think I can."

He saw who it was and started walkin' out toward my horse. He said, "Ben, that's the Cleveland bay horse that ole man Buck Hill traded that undertaker in on a bill because none of his cowboys could ride him. How come you with 'im?"

I said, "It's a long, painful story."

"Well, git down and spend the night and you can tell me all about it."

I told him I was pretty stiff and if this ole horse jumped as I started off, I might hang in the stirrups, and for him to reach up and git a hold of his bridle and twist one ear, and I'd try to git off. Ross was a good fellow, and we fed my horse and put him away and there was a whole lot less buck in him than there was when we started.

It was already late when I got there, but Ross's wife got up and fixed me a big supper and showed me where to go to bed. Ross and I visited a little while before we turned in.

When I took my britches off, the hide was gone on both legs from the top of my boots plumb up past my knee joints, but I thought a night's rest might cure a lot of that and it didn't take me long to get to sleep. It didn't seem like I'd been asleep for any time when I heard some pots and pans and noises around in the kitchen like country folk make that get up and cook and eat 'fore daylight.

I eased up on the side of the bed, got my boots and britches on and finished dressing, and found that I could stand up. By this time I'd decided I was goin' to live after all that buckin', and the smell of ham and hot biscuits comin' from the kitchen began to give me a new interest in life.

After breakfast, Ross helped me saddle the horse that I forgot to ask if he was broke. He looked worse'n I did. Sweat was dried all over him, the hard ride had caused the hair to slip under the cinch on him, and you could tell that when we started out he was a soft, overkept horse. That's where I had it on him. I was hard as iron and used to ridin'.

He didn't act like he was goin' to let me get on, so Ross put an extra rope around his neck and ran the rope through his mouth and back around under his chin and twisted it a couple of times. This gave him a more reasonable outlook on the possibilities of me ridin' him again, and I took my time about gettin' on him. I finally got set down on them sore places and clenched my raw knees against the saddle and told Ross to turn 'im loose. I had his head pulled up and he didn't offer to buck.

I cut across the country to Weatherford that day and the next day I rode back to Granbury. I don't know whether the folks in Granbury thought they would ever see me again or not, but by the time I rode in on the square, I had this used-to-be-badhorse drawed to about the shape of a greyhound. (In three days we'd been about a hundred miles.) He was un-shod and his feet had broken off in a few places to the quick and he was feelin' his way across the gravel where I was goin' to tie him to that courthouse chain. It had been a hard three days, but to have this good horse under me broke was worth all the pain and trouble.

I stepped down on the ground and as I started across to the drugstore, I tried to act like I was as fresh as a cowboy goin' to a square dance. I glanced over my shoulder and here was comin' Mr. Undertaker doin' the single-foot, and four or five more people had started toward the drugstore. I hadn't got to the soda fountain when Mr. Undertaker called my name in a very harsh tone. When I glanced around, several of my friends were standin' around lookin' and listenin' and deathly silent.

Mr. Undertaker's neck swelled and his face turned red, his voice was tuned high and sounded full of mad when he started in. "That mare has stood in one place and kicked all the spokes out of my hack, broke the shafts out of it, and tore up the harness. And you guaranteed her to work. What are you going to do about having my hack repaired and bringing me a horse to work?"

I smiled and reached over to the fountain for a drink of water the soda skeet had set out and very slowly turned around and said, "Mr. Undertaker, I guaranteed the mare not to run away!"

FAST
MULE BUYER

It was midwinter and the horse and mule market was at its most active best. I had been shippin' several carloads of mules a week to my customers over in the Mississippi Delta and in the southern states and had taken the time with this last shipment to get in my car and beat the train to its points of destination and help my customers unload their mules and do a little socializin' and public relations in order to keep more orders comin'.

I got orders from customers in Georgia for three carloads of good-aged, good-fleshed, small cotton mules to weigh from eight to nine hundred pounds each, which was the kind of mule that it took for the sandy land of Georgia.

Then on my way back, I stopped in the Louisiana sugarcane country and got an order from an old customer for a load of sugar mules. A sugar mule was one of the better class of nice well-turned-out mules that would weigh about eleven hundred pounds and show a good deal of style and quality.

On up in Arkansas some sawmill operators gave me an order for a carload of big, young, sound mules that were to be used in the lumber camps around the sawmill. Any mule buyer with orders for five carloads of mules is very much in business, so I was anxious to get back to Fort Worth for the Monday opening market.

I stopped in Cumby on Thursday night and stayed with my folks. I hadn't been to bed very much in several months and my eyes were givin' me some trouble, mostly from night driving I guess, so Friday I went in to Greenville and my old friend Dr. Strickland tested my eyes. He told me he would send off the prescription and if I

would wait until Monday morning, I could pick up my new glasses. There wasn't a whole lot I could do in Fort Worth over the weekend, so I thought I would visit with my folks, get some rest, and wait for my glasses.

I was up in Strick's office Monday morning when he brought in his mail and, sure enough, he had my glasses. He put 'em on me and I made some right smart horse-tradin' remarks about them windshields and he said, "They'll feel so good that you'll get to like 'em."

I paid him and broke off for Fort Worth. I sat up straight and spurred hard and got there just after the market opened and the auction was in full swing. I walked into the auction and shook hands and said my howdies with a few friends, but was careful not to wave my hand or nod my head in view of the auctioneer.

I watched thirty or forty mules sell. Wad Ross was sittin' in the auction box as he usually did. Jim Sheldon and old Bill Rogers were the auctioneers and they were taking time about selling the mules. It seemed to me that the morning's stock was pretty good in quality, flesh, and age, with not too many blemishes, and the market was about $15 to $20 a head cheaper than it had been two weeks before, so I set in to buyin' mules.

I bought about a half a carload of the Georgia cotton mules almost without competition and I noticed Wad gettin' real careful about callin' blemishes and ages and havin' them written on the ticket. Parker Jamison was working as ring man and he was sure givin' me a lot of attention. Of course, the auction never stopped for dinner and about three o'clock I had nearly a carload of Georgia cotton mules, half a carload of sugar mules, and a full carload of lumber mules and was by far the fastest and biggest buyer of the day so far.

I was a smart young mule buyer, but I had been at it long enough to know that there would be mules left after my money ran out since they had announced during the sale that the day's run would be about fifteen hundred head. So I decided I would stop long enough to eat a sandwich and drink a Coke at the stand there by the auction and then go down the alley and look at my mules I'd bought.

They had already assigned me three different pens for the different classes of mules that I was buyin', and as the auctioneer dropped the hammer on each mule, a messenger boy would bring me a copy of the ticket. It was the custom of the trade that sometime during the day, you would go down the alley to where your mules were penned and inspect each mule against the description on its ticket. If a mule's age had been misrepresented or if there were scars or blemishes that had not been called and written on the ticket, the bidder had the privilege of rejecting that mule. Rejects were then sold after all the fresh stock were sold and naturally brought less money than they had in the first go-around.

Denny was helping me with my mules, and as he turned the pen of Georgia cotton mules out on the plank-floored alley for us to catch and look at, I realized that it was a good deal darker in the barn alley than it had been in the auction ring. Since I wasn't used to glasses, I was catchin' some shadows and reflections, so I reached up and pulled off my glasses. I leaned up against the fence and watched these mules for a few minutes; they suddenly lost half a hand in height and about a hundred and fifty pounds in weight from what they had appeared to be in the auction ring. I knew my judgment hadn't slipped that much and it began to dawn on me that I had raised the market from $15 to $25 a head on the classes that I was buyin' and that was why Wad was watchin' the tickets so closely. As a nervous gesture, I put my glasses back on and them damn mules suddenly gained their height and weight that they had lost when I took my glasses off!

My lumber mules would do for sugarcane mules, my sugarcane mules were about the right size for my Georgia cotton mules, and my Georgia cotton mules were about the right size for a clown or mine mules, but I didn't have any orders for either one. And my new glasses that Strick had been so reasonable on had suddenly cost me about a $1,000.

THE
SHIELD
MARES

Old man Charlie Krinskey came through the barn at the San Antonio Horse and Mule Market just before the auction sale was to start and said, "Yeah, Ben, I see that you're lookin' at those fine old horses. The Shield horses, you know, have been famous for many years in this country."

The two horses that I was looking at were branded with a shield on the left hind leg about the level of the point of the flank, and I remembered that I had seen horses with this brand before. I saw that

the legs of these horses showed signs of much abuse, but when you looked at their withers and their backs and their beautiful loins and their good hindquarters, when you noticed the set of their ears and the width between their eyes, you couldn't help but wish that you'd had a horse like this when he was a four-year-old.

Now a man that spends his life horseback—and starts at a tender age—develops a keen eye for a good horse. He is ever in search of one that is better than the horse he has under him, or even better than the ones he is trying to breed at home. When the clothes he wears and the very meat and bread that go into his mouth are earned with, by, or from a horse, a man gets pretty sharp about horses. And I've been in tight spots with wild cattle and bad horses, spots where what my horse could do within the next few seconds would determine how well I would enjoy the next gasp of breath. So with such a background, I asked, "Mr. Krinskey, where do these horses come from, and why don't we see more of them?"

Down on the Rio Grande, he told me, there was a family that had bred these horses for many generations. They branded a shield on the shoulder of the mares and a shield on the hindquarter of the horses, and he had never seen a sorry one. But he had heard that the breed was running out, the old horse-members of the family had passed on and it would just be a matter of time until the Southwest would lose another strain of fine horses.

There was a severe drouth in the Southwest, it had been hanging on for several years. Cattle and horses had been sold off in great droves, and there wasn't too much live-stock left in the country. There had been no demand for broodmares. All men that were working livestock rode geld-ings. All the remudas at chuck wagons were geldings, and mares were seldom used for anything but to raise colts. Charlie and I talked about that, too.

He said, "Yeah, not much attention is gittin' paid to 'em,

and the broodmares of the country are gittin' sorrier as auto-mobiles are gittin' more plentiful."

Of course, when he mentioned automobiles it was just kind of a passing word. They hadn't cut too deep into the horse business; no such thing as a tractor existed to my knowledge; and nobody was too much worried about the future of the horse. We just assumed that we'd always have to have thousands of them and that they would be with us forever.

I stood looking over the fence as Charlie walked on down through the barn, and it just kinda occurred to me that if some young man had taken over the Shield that wasn't too interested in the horse business, this might be the place for me to get some broodmares better than I had ever owned. I thought about this all morning, made further inquiry, and learned a little about the way to get to the Shield Ranch. The best I could gather, it must be about two hundred miles —and I thought it would be a worthwhile trip to see if there were any Shield mares with all the many generations of good breeding in them that I could own at a reasonable figure and maybe keep myself mounted for the rest of my life. Horsemen are inclined to ramble like this in their thinking. Had it not been so, there would not have been developed such great breeds of horses as mankind has enjoyed through the years.

Next morning I loaded my saddle and the rest of my riggin' on a passenger train to Uvalde, Texas. This was get-tin' pretty far down in the big steer and brush country—ranches got bigger and fences got fewer. I got off the train in Uvalde and went up to a fine old hotel of the west on the square where I stood around a little while and visited. I found out there was a man who had a trading yard down close to the stock pens by the railroad track. I moseyed off down there afoot and saw he had some good saddle horses—and some others, too. I picked out a good dun horse that had clean feet and legs and a good, stout, hard body. He was shod. You could tell he had been used and was hard on grain and would be able to carry a man a long ways.

When I asked the fellow that had the horses about buying a saddle horse, he pointed out two or three different horses to me and made me a talk about each one of them. I looked over at the dun horse and asked about him. "Well," this fellow said, "yes, he's a good horse, but he's a horse I use myself, and he wouldn't come too cheap."

He didn't know it, but I wasn't looking for one too cheap. I was looking for one that could go deep into the brush country and give a man a fair chance of getting back on the same horse he left on. We didn't haggle much. He priced the horse too cheap, so I bought it.

This fellow took me up to the hotel in a little Ford roadster and went back down to his pens. I saddled my horse and started off. The horse moved out nice and had a good, long, flat running walk. He had a good short back and carried me easy and felt stout under me. I could tell he was what I needed for the trip I had in mind. He was about fifteen hands high, weighed a thousand and fifty pounds, and had a smooth way of carrying himself. He stepped over the ground with a fair overreach and nodded his head a little bit. You could tell he was a good road horse.

I went by Swartz's General Mercantile and bought a stake rope, a yellow slicker, and some grub to wrap up in my slicker and tie on the back of my saddle. I headed out south and a little west of Uvalde, following on the east side of the Anacacho Mountains a narrow country road that I thought would get me to the Shield Ranch. The first night out I camped in the foothills of the mountains by a little creek. My horse staked out good—behaved himself and went to grazing. I made a little fire and fried some meat on the end of a stick, then I made my bed and went to sleep.

It was the fall of the year and a little chilly—good sleeping weather—however, I waked up before daylight. My horse was full and rested, standing asleep on three legs at the end of his stake rope. He still had plenty of grass within reach. I fixed a little breakfast, got an early start, and headed out over the divide—still going toward the Rio Grande country. This country was awfully dry. I had seen very little livestock, very few cattle and hardly no horses atall. A little after noon on this second day, I rode on the site of a great big wide gate with high gateposts and an arch between them over the top of the gate. On this arch was a wide slab of oakwood with a huge shield burned into it and the name "Broquel," the word for shield in Spanish, burned beneath the shield.

I turned in and rode several miles before I came in sight of the headquarters of the Shield Ranch. There were a number of houses and corrals and improvements, and some of the big old trees like an old, old headquarters would have. You could see the house had thick 'dobe walls and was tile-roofed, and the outbuildings around it were of similar construction. It had been a ranch headquarters for many, many years.

Of course, a man that had lived his life in the West and had been around lots of cow outfits would readily detect which one of those buildings was the cook shack. I rode up to the cook shack, tied my horse to the hitch rack, and about the time I stepped on the ground somebody from inside hollered, "Git down, tie yore horse, and come in"—all of which I did.

There was a great big old long dining room with a great big long table running down through the middle of it, benches on both sides, and a chair at the end of the table. The cook was one of those old-timey ranch cooks, old and fat and happy about it all. Some cowboys were working in the corrals down below the headquarters. They saw me ride up, and of course they kinda got their work caught up—whatever they were doing—and moseyed up to the cook shack to get a cup of coffee and some conversation and find out who the newcomer was.

The West was pretty polite in those days. Nobody asked

you too many questions. If you wanted to tell them, they
listened—but if you didn't, they didn't ask you. Three cowboys came in and got big tin cups of coffee and sat down on
a long bench and talked and visited and told about the
drouth—it looked like it was going to be a hard winter. I
told them how much of the country it covered, and some
other things they hadn't heard. In those days, there was not
too much communication, very few radios, and not too many
ways of getting news from the outside. They had heard,
though, that the drouth was widespread, and we talked about
all the cattle and horses that had been shipped and sold,
and so on. But they were still fishing around, trying to find
out who I was and what business I had in the country without asking.

After a while I told them that I bought horses, and that I
needed some that would make good polo horses or military
horses (the government in those days was always buying
horses for the cavalry), but everything I found had been
too poor or too old or too something—that I hadn't had any
luck, and I guessed that I'd head out through the west and
go toward Del Rio and turn north and come into San Angelo
in the next ten or fifteen days.

One of these cowboys eased up from astraddle the bench
he was settin' on and started out the door that went toward
the headquarters. Nobody noticed him, and he didn't say he
was aleavin', or acomin' back, or make any mention he had
been there. I noticed this but made no comment about it.
Pretty soon he comes back following a nice-dressed, soft
young man that you could tell had been staying in the shade
and out of the dirt. His boots had a shine on, and his britches
had a crease in them. And you could tell that his boots
weren't spur-marked, and that he didn't have too much sign
of chap leather on his britches either. I noticed all this right
quick. He was clean-shaved and his hands were smooth,
fingernails kinda long for a ranch hand.

In the West, a man never grew a fingernail. He had them

torn off by lariat ropes or reins, or chewed them off because the weather was bad, or something. When you saw a man with nice-kept hands, long fingernails, creases in his britches, and shine on his boots, you would know that he was either the owner of the outfit or was the boss's son or had married his daughter, that he wasn't a common cowboy.

This young man walked in and stuck out his hand and introduced himself. He was the young Mr. Collin that was running the Shield. And, of course, for the first time, I told my name and told him that I was drifting by and just stopped to take on a little of his hospitality. He said, "Fine. I hope the cook fed you, and you are welcome . . . ," and all that kind of stuff that went with the passing of the day in the old Southwest.

Everybody else got up and got their own coffee, but the cook brought him a cup. He lit a cigarette, sipped his coffee, looked out the window, and talked about how dry it was and how they'd had to sell their cattle, cut down on their livestock, and it looked like some of the cowboys were going to have to leave and find work somewhere else. He said he'd just almost have to quit running the ranch until it rained and the place could be put back on a profitable basis. He made all this conversation sound awful high-class. He said it in a nice, cultured tone of voice without any pain or chagrin or regret; it seemed like he was kinda looking forward to shutting the outfit down and going to town and spending the winter.

Directly he gazed off past my shoulder out the window like he didn't even see me and said, "One of the boys said that you were a horse buyer."

I said, "Well, I'd like to be—only I haven't found any horses to buy on this trip. They've all been too old, or too poor, or too something or another. I haven't found any horses that I thought I could sell to the cavalry—or to anybody else, for that matter."

"A lot of horses," he said, "have been sold here during

the drouth, and there are not many good horses left in the country. Most of what's left are yearlings and twos and unbroke horses and broodmares."

I knew all of that—and of course those were the classes of horses that weren't worth much money. There wasn't much demand for them. He went on to comment that he had a lot of yearlings, twos, and threes, enough to last the ranch several years without raising any more.

I thought to myself, this is going to be easier than I intended for it to be; he is already offering to sell me what I came after, and I haven't had to show my hand. So I told him that since I hadn't been able to buy anything else, I might ought to try to buy some broodmares instead of going back to the north part of the country without any horses at all.

He said he had about thirty broodmares in the canyon pasture which wasn't more than a mile from headquarters. We could see some of them from an automobile if I wanted to drive down there with him and have a look. Well, this showing you horses from an automobile was kind of a new fandangle way of doing things, but you could tell alookin' at him that he wasn't too anxious to go showing them to you horseback; so I told him I guessed that would be all right.

He had a Mexican boy get in the back seat of this big automobile with the top laid back and several spare tires mounted on the rear. It was sure a long, fancy rig. We went down and dropped off the rimrock, went through a gate, and drove into the canyon pasture. He drove kinda slow down in through some great big boulders and greasewood, prickly pear, and mesquite—there wasn't any grass in this pasture to speak of—and we found a few mares standing in the shade down in the lower part of the canyon. Sure enough, they had the shield on them, and they were those kind of solid-color mares with good feet and legs, clean heads, nice keen necks, and beautiful backs. He said they were the old

Shield mares, that they had bred them pure for many years, and they were a pretty good kind of horse.

I could tell right off he didn't really know how good they were. He's just had good horses all his life, and he hadn't had any experience trying to work stock ahorseback on a sorry horse or he'd never have been willing to sell these deep-bodied, ribby kind of good mares. We saw about eighteen or nineteen head of them before we got to the other end of the pasture, and right at the gate there were five more,— made twenty-four altogether. He told me he thought there were twenty-eight in the pasture, that he didn't remember, but that he could ask somebody (he called his name) at the headquarters when we got back. These mares were mixed ages. There were a few old mares in them; there were also some nice, bright-headed young mares. There weren't any colts left on these mares—evidently they had been weaned and taken off to some other pasture, and these mares had been put in the canyon pasture to make the winter. All the mares I saw showed to be bred and would drop foals in the early spring. We had not seen a stud; so I asked what sort of a stud they were bred to. He said the stud was an old horse of the same type as the mares, but he had died because at his age he could not stand the drouth.

As we went out the gate at the lower end of the pasture, I noticed there was a good set of working corrals, plenty big and tall with good swing gates, that would be a nice place to pen a bunch of horses and look at them—or do whatever you wanted to with them. We drove on back toward the house, and he didn't say much more about the mares.

We got to the cook shack where I had left my horse, got out, and went in and sat down at the table. He asked one of the older cowboys how many mares there were. This cowboy said there were twenty-eight head. I asked how many old mares there were. He said there were four old mares and the rest were either middle-aged or young mares. He talked about this mare and that mare being just a four-year

old, and another one that was seven, and so on. This kinda
tallied out with what I had observed when I was looking at
them. They were all solid colors. They weren't great big,
but they were very typy and carrying lots of balance and
body and good bone structure. And they were sound, clean-
legged kind of mares, having plenty of substance without
being coarse. I had secretly thought to myself that with
mares like this, I'd never be afoot the rest of my life.

Still no mention had been made about price, but, after
all, there wasn't really much demand or much sale for
mares, especially in a drouth. I thought surely they wouldn't
be very high. When he finally got around to pricing these
mares, he said that they were going to go out of the mare
business and that mare buyers were pretty scarce. He would
price them to me where I would try to buy them.

I asked, "What would that be?"

He said he would take $30 a head for them. Well, along
about then the average run of good ranch mares were
bringing $10 to $12 apiece. Young, broke mares sometimes
would bring twenty, but $30 for broodmares was sort of un-
heard of. I didn't flinch. I didn't show much weakness. I
wanted those mares worse than anyone else would ever
have wanted them; so I just sat there a few minutes and
didn't answer.

He said, "What's the matter? Did that chill your blood?"

I said, "No, not exactly, but that's an awful lot of money
for mares."

"Well, then," he said, "what do you think you would give
for them?"

I said, "I might give $25 a head for twenty-eight head, if
they're all just like the ones we saw."

Of course he said they were. And the old ranch foreman
said the mares were all of the same breeding and all close
kin. You could tell this young Collin wasn't too interested
in their breeding, but he said that since this was Friday, it
would be Monday before he could get them up and deliver

them in the pens to me—for $25 a head. If I wanted to buy them, I could pay him half of it in cash now and the other half when I got the mares.

Well, I tried to set like I was worrying about it. Of course I had long since known I was going to buy the mares, but I didn't want to seem too anxious. I might scare this young blade a little bit about that being a pretty high-price for horses. I walked over by the stove and tore a piece of sourdough bread out of a pan and chewed around on it. Finally I said, "Well, I don't know what they're worth, and I don't believe anybody else does. But I believe if you'll take it, I'll give it and we'll have ourselves a horse trade."

He said he hoped I would take the mares plumb out of the country. I told him I would, I'd take them back up into northwest Texas. So I gave him $350 in cash. I had about that much in one pocket, and I could pay him that without showing whether I had any more money or not.

In the conversation he had mentioned twice that I could come back Monday after the mares. I thought it was a little peculiar that he didn't invite me to just stay until they could get the mares in the corral for me Saturday or Sunday. He could furnish me some help, and I could drive them out from there. That would kind of be the custom of the West, but I wasn't going to let any little customs interfere with a good horse trade; so I told him that I would ride on over to La Rio, which was a little town over about another twenty miles, and that I would be back Monday to get my horses.

He counted the money. The cook and the cowboys sat and listened and watched, and nobody made any comment about the trade atall.

My horse had got his breath, and I had eaten a batch of that ranch grub around there. Beans, beef, and potatoes— that was the common diet about that time on ranches. There wasn't any refrigeration to speak of, and nobody bought any canned grub to feed cowboys. So I'd made out a big dinner on what I was used to, and told him that I guessed I'd water my horse at the windmill over there and drift into town. I thanked the cook for fixing me some chuck, said good-bye to the boys, shook hands with the Señor Capitan, Mr. Collin, and got on my horse and rode away.

As I stepped on my dun horse, young Collin mentioned that he was a good stout horse but didn't look like he would have much speed. I said that I hadn't had him long and hadn't tried him—he might not, I didn't know. I did notice that when the young Collin commented about my horse, one of those cowboys had just a little bit of a smile on one side of his face. Of course, everybody said something about one another's horses, and I didn't think much about it.

I rode into the little town of La Rio on the banks of the Rio Grande, way up high on the bluff and looking over into Old Mexico—a typical little bitty old border town. You wondered how it got built there and how it survived. But there were some people, and some business—a country store, a few other little buildings. Wasn't anybody around much it was nearly sundown, but dusk lingers in the dessert regions of the Southwest and it would be a good while before dark. At the back of this country store was a set of corrals to be used by anybody that rode in to spend a day or two in town. Whatever you might buy at the store, your horse or your team was handy there for you. Everybody just generally understood this, and a newcomer knew at a glance that this was the place to leave his horse. At the back side of the corrals there were some little old low sheds, and a few snarled old mesquite trees were in the middle of the corrals. The trees gnarled and you could tell by the bark on them that they had been rope-burned by broncs and that all kinds of horses had been tied to them. The leaves were picked off pretty high, like some old pony had stood there waiting for a rider that was spending a little too much time in town and had left him there to pick at the mesquite or starve. I tied my horse to one of these old trees.

Nobody was in sight. The door to the country store was

open, so I walked in to ask if it was all right to leave my horse there. A nice-looking, squatty old Mexican fellow said, "*Sí, señor*, you are welcome."

Then I said, "I guess I'll spend the night. I wonder if it would be all right if I make my camp there in the back of the corrals?"

"*Sí, señor*, 'most everybody that comes in horseback stays here. You are welcome."

I walked up the street a little piece to one of the few buildings on the same side of the street—facing north with the back of the buildings toward the bluff that overlooked the Rio Grande—and into the little café. It was a plain, dingy kind of place, but a nice-looking middle-aged man behind the counter said, "Come in. What's it for you?'"

I asked him what he had, and he named a thing or two. He could cook me some steak, or he had some chili all ready to serve. Eating there at the counter was a nice-looking white-haired old gentleman sitting straight and erect on a stool. He was slight of stature, but he had a very impressive profile. As I glanced at the food he was eating, I couldn't help but notice that his hands didn't look near as old as his body. To a cowboy, this would mean that there was a man who, even though he had spent his life in the saddle as a rancher and a stockman, hadn't been given to any menial chores. His hands weren't knotted or gnarled up by post-hole digging, moving rock, or the common labor that boogers up a man's hands as time goes on.

I sat down next to him and ordered a bowl of chili. On the wall was a sign that said, "Water, 5c a Glass." The drouth had robbed the little town of its water supply, and what water that was being used had to be hauled in quite a distance from some wells. There were wells, possibly, in the town that the natives shared with each other, but for water that had to be hauled to serve to a passer-by there was a charge. I glanced at the sign and said, "I'll need some water."

The café man put a goblet down—one of those heavy, old-timey kind that stand up on a stem—and poured it full of water. I noticed the old gentleman that I had sat down by, his glass was empty. I said, "And my friend would like another glass of water."

The old gentleman gave a quick sort of glance at me and said, "I thank you, sir," in the clearest, best English speech that I had heard in a long time.

I finished my supper and walked out on the street and back down to put my horse away. I realized then that I was going to have to figure out some way to water my horse. The mercantile store had turned on a dim light, so I walked in and asked if I could buy some feed for my horse, and where could I water him. The man said he had some oats and alfalfa, but that water was precious. At the back of the store he had a tank of water hauled up from the river. It wasn't quite fit for a man to drink but it was all right for horses. It was a quarter a tubful.

I said, "Well, I know my horse will drink a tubful."

He went to the back of the store to dip me some oats, and he got me two small chips of alfalfa hay from a couple of bales in a little lean-to on the back of the store. With the drouth, feed was scarce and money was scarce, and few people fed their livestock. They just changed horses and rode them on whatever they could find to eat—so, naturally, he didn't have a lot of feed on hand. Then he reached over and turned an old wheel on a pipe at the back wall of the store, and a tub on the outside began to fill with water. When I looked outside, the tub turned out to be a great big old wood tub made of hand-hewn wood stays bound by two wagon tires.

I unsaddled my horse and slipped the bit out of his mouth and just left one rein to go around his neck to lead him around to his tub of water. He drank about half of it, and I heard a sort of half-nicker from a horse in the small corral behind me. I looked up. The old gentleman that I had eaten beside at the café was walking out to his horse, which was an unusual individual, just like the man who owned him. This was a horse of much substance with a good topline and good legs, heavily muscled hindquarters, and gathering muscles along his back and his belly that you might say were overdeveloped. He was a horse that showed to have had much use—and much care, too. His feet were in good condition, his mane and tail combed. He had been ridden hard. The hair was short over his loins where the saddle rubbed. The hair had been worn off on the side where his cinch fit him. No sores, no scars, no blemishes—just the hair cut away by constant use of the cinch. I couldn't help but admire such a useful-looking horse—neither young nor old, but a horse in his best using years, something like ten or twelve years old.

Of course he had nickered when he smelled that tub of water and heard my horse drink, and I said to the old gentleman, "I think my horse could learn things just standing across the fence from yours. There's more water here than my horse will drink and I'd be glad for your horse to have it, if you would care to water him after my horse."

"It is his thirst that causes me to accept," said the old gentleman.

He let down the drawbars and turned the horse loose to come to the water trough without a rope on him. The more you looked at the horse, and the more you looked at the man, the more you wondered about them. This was the darkest colored chestnut horse that you nearly ever saw. The man stood there beside him while he drank, a hand on his withers. I saw him pinch the withers, and the horse raised his head and stood there a minute—corrected for not having proper manners at the trough and drinking too fast. It was very noticeable to me that this man had complete control of the horse just with the use of his fingers on his withers.

There was plenty of water, and when his horse finished, the man turned and walked back through this drawbar gate.

The horse came in behind him. I said, "A horse with that much sense, I guess could take those drawbars down if he chose to."

The old gentleman gave a light, pleased sort of smile. It was the first time I had seen the expression change on his face at all. He said, "I see you do appreciate a good horse."

"Yes, I do. He's a much better horse than the one I am riding."

He answered, "You are probably mounted well enough for whatever distance you must travel." A polite but curt kind of a statement, spoken in a clear, proper tone with each word clipped sharp to fit in place.

I wondered where he came from and how come he was in the Southwest where everybody slurs and slangs the language; but I said, "Well, I guess I'd better make my camp somewhere around under one of these sheds."

He said, "Move over to the south side with me. On top of the bluff there is some breeze which will be pleasant during the evening."

I hesitated a minute. Cowboys don't hear night called evening very often, and not from another horseman, anyway. I picked up my saddle and bedroll and followed him over to the shed that faced south. It looked out over the river—that was dry—across the bleak old desert into Old Mexico. Far in the distance the rugged Huachuca Mountains loomed up out of the blue of the desert twilight.

I spread out my saddle blanket, took off my boots, and stretched out with my head on my saddle. He leaned back against a post, and we sat there mostly in silence. Finally I mentioned the drouth.

He said, "Yes. The drouth is severe in my country, too."

I thought this would be my best opportunity, and I asked, "And where would that be?"

"In the heart of the Huachuca Mountains about five days' ride into Mexico. Our land is very dry. Our herds have long since gone. I came to this country to seek employment, for I must provide for my people."

We sat in silence again. The coolness of the desert began to rise up from below and the fresh night air was getting chilly. In spite of drouth, in spite of the heat of the day, the desert is always a place to sleep in comfort through the night. By now the noises of the night, even though they were few, had become noticeable. There was a nice steady cool breeze blowing. We could hear our horses cleaning up what hay and grain we had given them, and it was a very peaceful scene.

This man I had met in such an odd sort of way—over a drink of water—was somewhat puzzling to me. As I lay on my pallet, I could study his profile in the moonlight—the way he leaned back against that post. His features were chiseled according to the pattern of aristocrats and monarchs. His eyes were large and dark and very expressive. His hair was snow white and lay heavily on his head in a slight wave over the top and curled up some at the back of his hat. His selection of words was proof that he had an unusual background, entirely different from that of most people in this part of the United States and Mexico. I was very anxious to know more about him; but he hadn't inquired into my affairs, my background, or my purpose in being in the Rio Grande country. I didn't feel that he had given me any reason to ask him any personal questions. I didn't want to cause him any embarrassment or make him ill at ease over some question that he might not care to answer, so I thought I would bide my time. The night was young, and tomorrow was a new day.

I murmured to my companion that I thought I would doze off and take a nap. He responded by saying, "Then I shall retire, also." There was some more of that wording. He didn't say, "I believe I'll take a nap," or "get unconscious," or "wallow out a place," or "snooze," or any of those things that sleep is described with by men of the range.

To say that a man "looked like he had spent his life in the saddle" didn't describe him in the Southwest, because we all had. You could come nearer to describing an individual and setting him apart if you said he hadn't spent his life in the saddle. For the most part, a man that spent his life in the saddle—with the age that this man had—was stiff and bowlegged and maybe walked with a limp. Many were stooped in the shoulders. Those that had other hard labor to do, such as building fence or menial chores that didn't belong to horseback endeavor, would have injured hands and big knuckles and maybe an enlarged or stiffened wrist.

A close study of this individual showed that, even though he was from Mexico, he was not a Mexican. Neither could it be said that he belonged to the Anglo-Saxon race. His appearance and speech were baffling to a wild rough cowboy that didn't know a whole lot about the human race anyhow. This man showed no signs of ever having done any hard labor or menial chores. His hands were smooth, and the manner in which he used them was very impressive. It is true that he was bowlegged and a little stiff in the joints, but his back was very erect and there was a bit of movement in his shoulders that isn't common to men that have done all sorts of hard work.

By now I had run all this through my mind and was fast on my way to drifting off to sleep and getting some rest and being refreshed for another day. The days you spend—be they hard, long, hot, or dry—are bearable if you sleep at night. Cowboys learn this at an early age, and they usually keep the habit as long as they live.

About daylight I rolled over, rose up, and wiped my eyes, and remembered how come I was there. I'd had a good night's rest, and the world was beginning to come alive in a sleepy sort of way. I looked about me, and my companion of the night was standing up very straight, looking out across the desert into Mexico. He didn't seem to know that I had waked up, and I said, "Are you trying to see what they are doing at home?"

He was a serious sort of individual, and he answered, "I can well imagine the duties being performed this hour by my people in the heart of the Huachuca Mountains."

I said, "It sounds as if you wish you were home."

"I have been away many months, and I should like to return. In fact, I only stopped here to rest my horse and to procure supplies. I shall leave in a day or two. I hope to be on my own lands within the week to come."

I put on my clothes, pulled my boots on, got up and stretched, and said, "Well, I guess I'd better see about my horse."

He said, "I have fed your horse and mine from the feed that you purchased yesterday afternoon."

"Thank you. I appreciate it."

He said, "It is strange, but I must assume that I had the feeling toward feeding your horse that you had last evening toward watering my horse—not a personal thing between one man and another, but a feeling for the horses. It was not intended as a gesture to make you feel obligated, sir."

"Well," I said, "thanks anyway. When do you suppose that place opens up where we ate last night? I'd like to have some breakfast."

"It is Sunday morning. I doubt that he will open soon."

There was no water to drink, no place to wash our faces and hands, and I said, "Well, I'd think a man that's in the café business ought to open up early any day."

"I hope that you are correct in your thinking." His phraseology had no breaks or lax places. It was amazing to hear him talk, and in such light, curt, well-chosen and well-pronounced words.

I walked over to the front part of the corral to my horse, ran my fingers through his mane, and scratched his back a little bit. I picked us a piece of mesquite wood about the size of a curry comb and rubbed it around over his back to break the dry hair from yesterday's sweat. I rubbed up and down his legs a little with my hands, just to see if he was all right—and to reassure him that he w?s being looked after. After all, who knows but what a cow horse appreciates a little extra attention. When you live with a horse, you care more for him and you see more about him than you do if you ride him only on Sunday.

I glanced out across the street and saw the fat man coming up the hill, the one who owned the café. I thought to myself that we would get breakfast, even if it was Sunday. I gave him time to get to his place of business while I curried and brushed my horse. Then I walked back to the back of the corral where we had slept and where my friend was—I still didn't know his name—and I said, "I saw the café man pass, and he's had time to open up. Would you join me in some breakfast?"

He turned and looked at me rather pleased but neither with surprise nor alarm nor any of those rank, wild things you use to describe a man's expression. He said, "That would be most enjoyable."

We walked out of the corrals together and up the street a piece to where this little café was. Sure enough, the door was open and you could smell coffee was beginning to boil. The café man was getting ready for his day's business. First thing I wanted was a big drink of water; so he set out some of those big goblets and filled them with water out of a crock pitcher. We drank our water, and then he served the coffee. Of course in a little country café, there are just three or four things they fix for breakfast and everybody knows what they are. In that day nobody every printed a menu or knew how to spell the words. I ordered some ham and eggs, and my friend ordered some eggs and some hash-browned potatoes. I said, "Don't you want some meat, too?"

He answered, "I don't care for porcine flesh." In other words, he didn't eat hog meat—but that was a very elite way of putting it, I thought, between two cowboys in a country café on the Rio Grande banks. Maybe he didn't know how else to say it.

We finished breakfast, and for want of anything else to do, we started walking back toward the corrals. I said, "Well, it's Sunday and it's going to be a long day."

"Are you riding far?" This was the first question he had asked me.

"No, sir. I've got to wait until Monday and receive some horses."

He said, "I think I shall not ride out today, either."

So for want of something else to do, we walked up and down the dry bed of the Rio Grande. He commented on the shapes of rocks, the lay of the terrain, and how the mountains rose up out of the desert. You could tell that he had a vast store of knowledge; his conversation was interesting, but it was highly impersonal and spoken very correctly. This was a new breed of man to me. I tried to talk cattle with him, but he wound up the subject with a well-selected phrase. It was hard for me, a cowboy, to start much of a conversation with him; so about noon we drifted back up to the one little street of the town and on toward the eating place.

There were very few people stirring. We heard the bell ring and saw a few people on their way to church, the ladies with white lace shawls and the men in white shirts. I said nothing of religion and neither did he. When we walked into the café there were a few other men there but no ladies at all. I paid for dinner, and as we walked out on the street, he said, "I have imposed considerably upon your hospitality in partaking of food for which you have paid."

I said, "It is my pleasure to be with a man who is so well informed and who is such pleasant, clean company. I am more than repaid. Think nothing of it." This was the first outburst of politeness that he had heard from me, and it seemed to impress him very much. He looked at me in a more appraising manner than he had before. We were about even with the corrals when I said to him, "I'll be glad to get those broodmares tomorrow and get on my way back toward the Northwest." Then we came on up by his horse and I said, "This horse has good balance and mighty good legs."

"You have a keen eye for a horse."

"Yes, sir," I said, "I've had to have. I've lived horseback— made my living with horses—but this horse puzzles me almost as much as you do. He's not a horse of thoroughbred breeding; he's not an Arab; and he's certainly not a mustang horse. I admire him very much. He's unusual, even to the brand on his hind leg. It's a brand that I would interpret as a tree."

"Yes, the brand is a tree, and he is truly a well-bred horse." And that was just about all he said. He cut it off with that.

I thought I had baited him enough that he might tell me something about himself or about his horse—but he didn't. We sat down in the shade of the shed where our saddles and beds were. I leaned back against my saddle and looked out across the desert toward the mountains in Mexico. Finally he broke the silence by saying, "You said you bought some broodmares."

"Yes, sir. I'm going to take them to my ranch up close to Fort Worth."

"From whom did you purchase these mares?"

Well, he had begun to ask questions. I thought I'd tell him something and maybe he would tell me something. I said, "I bought the mares from the Shield Ranch."

His eyes narrowed and his mouth dropped open a bit, and he said, "You, too, have bought those mares."

I pondered a bit to analyze his statement, and then I asked, "Who else has bought them?"

"My young friend, these mares have been sold many times, but a purchaser has never been able to get them off the ranch."

I said, "I bought them to be delivered in the corrals of the canyon pasture."

"Alas, that is the way they have been sold to many other men."

I had left three hundred and fifty dollars at the Shield Ranch and that, all of a sudden, bothered me. I knew this man had no humor about him; he wasn't fixing to pull a joke on me. I asked, "Would you explain the meaning of your statement? It puzzles me. I have bought the mares and paid half the purchase price."

"I assumed so," he said. "That is the usual arrangement."

"Well, what's wrong? They are, I thought, exceptionally good mares."

"They truly are exceptionally good mares," he agreed.

"Then you know the horses?"

"Yes," he said, "I know the horses, and I know the horses from which they were bred. My young friend—your hospitality, your kindness, and your company cause me to call you friend"—I could tell by the way he used the word that it was significant to him, that he didn't pitch it around lightly, and that he had finally decided to be my friend—"my young friend, the young Collin is a rascal. He has used these mares to gain money from others. It is true that your judgment of a horse is good. The Shield mares are the best along the Rio Grande for hundreds of miles. It is also true that they will deliver them into the corrals to you, but only a hired hand will be there, or perhaps the cook. You will pay the balance of your money and turn the mares out of the corrals into a big pasture to drive them to the public road a distance of about five miles. You will pass through a canyon and some very rough country, heavily wooded country with catclaw, greasewood, mesquite brush, and huge cactus plants. It is through this rough country that the mares will lose you. They will scatter and run. They know the range. They know the trails. They know how to get away; therefore, a buyer never gets to the public road with these mares. For three years, this has been the story of the sales of these mares.

"While you are trying to gather your wild mares, the young Collin will be in Del Rio or San Antonio spending the part payment you have made on these horses. Perhaps, after many months, he will return half of your money to buy the mares back from you. Then again, he may say that since you have not taken the mares, you no longer own them."

I didn't doubt a word this gentleman said. I listened carefully. He could tell that I was worried, and I could tell that he was concerned. He offered no sudden advice, and he offered no criticism. He did say, "You are not well enough mounted to outcourse the Shield mares, to hold them in herd or to drive them to the outside gate. How much money did you leave with young Collin?"

"I paid him three hundred and fifty dollars."

"That is much more than others have paid him. However, the mares are worth more than twice this amount if you can get them off the Shield Ranch and to the public road."

I said, "I'll need to hire some other riders. Would you go with me and help gather the mares? We'll get some more cowboys."

"I doubt that you can hire local men. They know of this trade. They will not risk offending the young Collin by driving these mares."

I realized that this old gentleman knew much about the customs of the country and the men that inhabited it, but I didn't yet care to question him as to how come he knew all these things.

I heard a noise over toward the mercantile. The old merchant was opening up for a while on Sunday afternoon. When he opened up the back door I said, "I'll go to the store and buy some more feed and water for our horses."

My friend—we'd gotten that far, he'd called me friend—didn't comment or make any sort of answer, and I walked on over to the store to pay for some more alfalfa hay and another tubful of water. From the back door, I went over to the corral and pulled down the drawbars for my friend's horse to drink. He got up and stepped with considerable haste over to take care of his horse. He made no comment about my turning his horse out to drink, but you could tell he appreciated it and didn't want the horse to be any bother to me. He stepped between my horse and his and stood there by his horse's neck while they drank. The water was still gushing out of the pipe. It was cool even though it wasn't the best of water, but it was the best that could be had around there for horses.

Both horses seemed to enjoy their fill. He patted his on the shoulder, and the horse walked back into the corral. I led my horse back and took his bridle off. Both went to munching what little hay they had left. I know I must have been wearing a worried look on my face because my friend turned to me and said, "I have decided that this time the Shield mares will be delivered to the purchaser."

"Do you mean that you are gonna help me?"

"Yes."

"How many more men will we need?" I asked.

"None. You and I shall receive them."

This was the first time he had phrased me into a sentence with himself, and I took note of that. He said, "We shall need several hundred feet of small rope. You should purchase it now in order that I may fashion it to our purpose."

I didn't question him. I said, "Well, let's go into the mercantile store and you pick out the rope that we'll need."

In those days, rope was laid out in coils under the counter. The end of the rope ran through a hole bored in the front of the counter; so you pulled the rope through the hole and unwound whatever amount that you wanted from those big coils. And there were many sizes and kinds of rope; so you walked along the front side of the counter and looked at these rope ends that were sticking out of the holes in the front of the counter. He picked out a very small, tightly woven, quarter-inch rope. He said, "This will be ideal."

"How much of it will we need?"

"How many mares are there?"

I told him twenty-eight, and he said, "Ten feet—two hundred and eighty feet—perhaps three hundred feet."

The old man was standing behind the counter watching and listening to us, but he hadn't made any comment. I said to him, "We need three hundred feet of this quarter-inch rope."

All old counters in those days had some tacks hammered in the counter to mark off three-feet, six-feet, and ten-feet measures of rope. The storekeeper came around to the front side of the counter and went to measuring off the rope. He got to three hundred feet and, as the custom was, he jerked three or four more feet to be sure you were getting good measure.

I asked, "How much money?"

"Three cents a foot, *señor*."

So I paid him nine dollars out of my pocket, and by this time my friend had the coil of rope over his arm and was started out the back door. As we approached the shed where we were camping, he asked, "Who else knows that you have purchased the Shield mares?"

"Nobody else. Nobody has asked, and there's been nobody around to tell, anyhow."

He said, "Be sure that you speak no more of this trans-action." And he sat down and went to cutting the rope into ten-foot lengths.

I said, "That's awful small rope to hold a horse."

"Have no fear, my friend." And after he had the rope all cut, he began to plat beautiful little square knots in the ends of the rope—one knot in each end of each ten-foot length.

I said, "This is going to take lots of time. Why don't you just tie these knots in here?"

"We have the time. How else might I spend the after-noon?"

It was a small rebuke, for which I said, "I'm sorry."

"It is nothing. You may watch me." And I watched him. With those long, slender, effective fingers, he platted square knots into that quarter-inch rope about as fast as I could have tied them using a common knot. "Common knots," he said, "will come undone and permit the rope to ravel. A square knot platted will stay secure and will be more to our purpose. It affords an easy grasp."

I just grinned and said, "I'm glad you know what you're doing. I don't."

He made no reply, but by now it was middle-afternoon, and I thought if the café was open that I would get him some coffee. I said, "I think I'll mosey around a bit."

"Yes. You have some walking to do in order that you may rest tonight." This was the first suggestion of humor that I had ever heard in his speech.

I walked up to the café and had a cold drink that wasn't very cold. It was iced sparingly because ice came once a week on the train. I took some coffee back to my friend in a fruit jar, and he sipped on it and finished the rope a little before dark.

Next morning we had a quick breakfast, saddled our horses, and set out in a nice, flat walk. We didn't hurry our horses, and we got there about the right time of day. We rode up to the corrals and, sure enough, the mares were in the corrals. Nobody was around. He stopped and surveyed the situation and told me to ride on up to heaquarters and take my time, but it would be best if I could transact my business and not let anybody come back to the corrals with me. He said that of course they wouldn't want to—other than they might enjoy seeing the mares break and go back into the wilds of the pasture. But outside of that, they'd have no cause to want to watch me try to move the horses.

I rode up to the headquarters, and there was no sign of life anywhere until the cook stepped out on the porch and spoke to me. He said that Señor Collin and all the cowboys were at another part of the ranch, but that he had been given instructions to take the money for the rest of the payment on the horses. I got down off my horse and counted it out to him standing on the porch. He asked if I would come in and have a bit to eat, but I told him that I had brought a little grub with me rolled up in a sack behind the saddle, and that I'd go on back and get ready to drive my horses to town.

He said, "Oh, that'll be fine," but you could tell he was a little amused. "Did you bring anyone to help you?"

I said, "I guess there's nobody here at the ranch to help me to the road with these mares." I didn't really answer his questions, but it sounded to him like I was alone.

"I suppose there should be," he said, "but all the boys left early this morning."

As I stepped on my horse and turned him back down toward the corrals, I noticed a cowboy's shadow on the window of the bunkhouse—but I didn't turn to look. I just rode on. The corrals were between the main headquarters and the public road and off to one side from the regular road maybe half a mile. As I rode up, I saw about half of the mares wearing a little rope tied around their necks right at the throat latch—up close behind their ears and just under their jaws—just as close as a throat latch would fit if it were coming off a bridle. These little ropes were drawn up tight, not enough to choke, but there was a fold of skin drawn up under the rope—no slack and no air at all between the rope and the mare's neck, not even room to pass your finger.

My distinguished friend was catching these mares—they were gentle to catch—and putting these little ropes on them with a slip knot that had a little knot tied under it. He explained to me that these little ropes were just exactly as tight as a horse could breathe at a walk, but when the horse started to run and had to expand her nostrils and windpipe, then these ropes would choke. And while the mare was choked, she couldn't run. She would gasp for breath and stagger. This would make it possible for us to ride around these mares and herd them back in a bunch to drive to the road.

I had never heard of this trick, but it made sense. He explained to me that it was an old trick that he had learned in Mexico, and that for once the Shield mares were not going to scatter like a covey of quail when they hit the greasewood, mesquite, and cactus. When these mares tried to run, the extra breath they needed would cause them to choke down. We would have no difficulty driving them to the road.

He said that when we got them to the road that he could give them relief. This didn't make sense to me—this relief —but all the rest of his plan sounded foolproof, even though I had never seen it tried or heard of it before. Anyway they showed very little fright when he would rope them or walk up and catch them. At the last there were three or four that we had to crowd in behind a gate—push against the fence and turn the gate back against them—in order to reach through the cracks of the fence and tie the little rope on them.

When we had the last rope on the twenty-eighth mare, he had two ropes left over. He said he didn't know why he needed an extra, but that it had always been his custom to have an extra rope or two at anything he might undertake in handling horses, which would make sense in anybody's language. He led his horse into the corral, drove the mares up close to the gate, and told me to open the gate and ride out in front of them—in the hope that they would follow my horse if they didn't choose to run. Well, 1 opened the gate and held my horse up to just a modest trot, and he waved his hands and spoke to the mares. As they came out at the gate, there was a little flat in front of the corrals—oh, maybe a quarter to a half mile long—and it was in this little flat that you could drive them a little piece. It was when they hit the brush on the other side that they would break and get away from you.

We were about halfway across this little flat when the

Shield mares all decided to go to the hills. And when they did, they ran past me. He hollered at me in a loud tone of voice to run the mares. He was running all that he could, and he had one of those little ropes in his hand. He would ride up and slap a mare with this rope. Of course it had no sting to it—it was so light and all—but mares that had been on the range, it would cause them to try to run away. In less time than it takes me to tell this, we had the mares strangled and choked and staggering around on the flat, and they were scattered over no more than three or four acres.

We rode around them and whipped them into a bunch and started off with them again. When they got to the edge of the greasewood and mesquite, they made another wild run to leave. Some of them fell to their knees, others just stood spraddle-legged and gasped for breath; but the harder they tried to run, the more their throats expanded and the worse they choked. We had some mares get down, but not for more than a few minutes. When they got down, they quit breathing so hard, and then they would come back up.

It was a broad, plain trail going to the gate. About the time the first mare started down it, the others began to bunch up behind her. By then I had my lariat rope out with about twenty-foot length of doubled rope—and he had his —and we could ride in and brand these mares with a hard lick if they tried to get out of the bunch. Once they began to get their breath, they were no trouble to drive. Oh, every now and then one would begin to break out, but she wouldn't go more than a few yards before she would begin choking. When she did, you could ride around her without any hurry and put her back in the bunch.

We were outside the gate in less than an hour and going down the public road. The mares were walking nice and slow, but some of them had broken out in a sweat—not from heat so much as from fright and lack of air. The old gentleman would ride up to a mare, and while that good horse of his walked alongside the mare, my friend would loosen the lock knot and slip the rope enough for the mare to breathe easily. By the time we had gone four or five miles, he had loosened the rope on each of the mares, and they were all trotting along perfectly at ease and getting all the wind they needed. But they were in a fenced road with no way to turn back and no way to get away.

For a while they traveled at a long, sweeping trot. We rode in a lope to keep up with them. These mares were unusual in their soundness of leg, wind, and limb—and in their body conformation, eyes, and heads. They were good horses, and I had noticed there was a marked resemblance between them and the horse my friend was riding. I hesitated to say anything about it. I had given him one opportunity to tell me about his horse, and he didn't; so I decided to bide my time further. I supposed I would learn about it later on, and in the meantime he had been all-wise in everything that he had done so far.

In the late afternoon we drove the mares into the corrals at the mercantile. There was no more than a dozen men standing up and down the streets, in the mercantile, and at the post office—but by dark there had been fully a hundred people by the corrals to look at these mares. Most of these people in the little town of Rio spoke Spanish. I understood some of it, but not all. But there was quite a lot of explanation and commotion and hand waving about the Shield mares.

I went to buy some hay, and the old man in the mercantile showed much surprise that the Shield mares were in his corrals. "I am glad to see them," he said. "Always I hear much about them, now I see the Shield mares. They are beautiful. Señor Boquel, before he departed this earth, was great horseman and many years my good friend."

The corral fences behind this old mercantile were in reasonably good condition. There was a gate on the east side and a gate on the north side in front. Only at these gates did you need to worry about a horse getting away. So we stretched lariat ropes across the gates and tied them shut at both ends. We also used the baling wire off the hay we were feeding to tie these gates securely. My gentleman friend picked up some tin cans and wired them loosely to the gates; then he picked up a few smooth rocks about the size of your thumb and dropped them in the cans. He said that any attempt to open the gates by a man or horse would rattle the cans and wake us up—and we would have plenty of time before anyone or anything could get those gates unwired.

All of this was wise, and these were things I had never heard of before in my horse experience. Of course it was an eye-opener for me to meet a man of such wide experience and such clean, true, distinct use of the English language. Now I admired 'most everything he did, and I listened carefully to everything he said. He had taken an extreme interest in my business and in saving the Shield mares for me, yet "rascal"—the word which he used to describe the young Collin—was the strongest term I had heard him use in the two days and nights we had been together.

We built a small fire, cooked some grub, and sat and watched the mares get settled down. The twenty-mile trip to town had jaded them some. They were quiet, and I talked about how good they were, and how proud I was of them, and what I intended to do with them in the way of establishing me a band of horses. All of this seemed to interest my friend, and then I asked him what I would owe him for his services. I didn't use the word work, or hire, or any of those common things. He was truly a genius at what he was doing, and he had rendered me more service than just being a hand.

He said that I had trusted him, and that he trusted me; that although he had little money—he had been conveying his money to Mexico while he had worked in this country—

he would prefer taking some of the Shield mares instead of being paid in cash.

I told him that sounded fair to me, and how many mares did he feel like he should have for his services? The brands looked like they had been blotched on some of the older mares, but they were all Shield mares, and he had seen the mares now as much as I had.

He told me that if I would travel west with these mares about twelve or fifteen miles the next morning, I could turn up a road to the north that would be a good road to drive these mares toward Fort Worth. He would help me on up to where this road turned off, and then he would turn south, cross the Rio Grande, and go into Mexico at almost the same point. On the road, we would talk more about what mares he wanted.

I told him that would be fine. After all, I didn't need over fifteen or twenty of these mares to establish a band of horses; I had thought about selling a part of them to get some of my money back, and we would discuss this as we went up the road tomorrow. I told him, too, that this had been a very unusual experience in my career as a horse buyer—to buy mares of this quality, and then to have found a man who knew so much about handling mares— and that I would never forget the things he had taught me on this trip.

His voice softened some toward me as he spoke. "It goes well with an older man when a young man is grateful to him for knowledge and help. I am glad that we met. This love of yours for good horses, it will perpetuate the Shield strain."

We went on to sleep, but sometime in the night I was awakened by the rattle of a can. I got to my feet, and I saw that he was halfway to the gate. It was only a mare rubbing against the gate and was no cause for alarm. Of course we both slept lightly, and we got up at daylight to start our trip as early as possible. There wasn't enough water at the store for my mares, and according to my friend, I could water my mares after I turned north on the road he suggested.

We turned the mares out in the road just at dawn. He rode on ahead and I brought up the tailin's as we drifted them to the outskirts of town. In just a little while we got to where there were no side roads, and he dropped back and we rode along together. The mares were leveled off walking. Everything was goin' rather smooth, and I thought this would be time to bring up about the mares he wanted. I asked him, "Which of the mares would you prefer, and how many?"

He said, "I think my time and labor would be worth one mare, and any of the mares would be good enough."

I said, "My friend, and that's the only name I know for you, your services are worth far more than one mare. I suggest that you pick two of your own liking. Their ages are about their only difference, but you choose whichever two mares you would rather have out of the bunch."

He must have been a little bit touched by my proposition. His voice softened some and he said, "I do not often pass out my name or my identification. The name 'friend' means a great deal when spoken in truth between horsemen. I am Don Ricardo Olivorez of the Tree Ranch in the Huachuca Mountains of Mexico." He paused, and then he said, "I'll tell you more. Several generations ago my people came to the New World from Spain. My ancestors were of noble birth and, experiencing difficulty with the Spanish regime, they decided to come to the New World and start their lives anew. They brought gold, acquired much land, and they brought a number of the purest of the Andalusian horses from the Andalusian mountain country of Spain.

"Both my grandfather and my father were schooled in Spain, as were other members of the family. Each time a family member went to Spain for his higher learning, he returned to the ranch with additional pure Andalusian horses from the mother country. When I was a young man, they sent me to Spain—and later to England. I was privileged to have the opportunity of much education, but in my lifetime it has been very difficult for the Olivorez family to support good government and at the same time stay in good graces with the powers in Mexico. I regret to explain, but there are times when good government and those in power are not the same."

He went on to say that his family lands had been sieged many times. The rancho had suffered greatly from taxes and various plundering expeditions, and the present drouth had almost been too much. Although my friend had come to the States to work, he told me that he was the first of the Olivorez family to have ever asked another man for employment.

He said, "The horse I ride is of the purest Andalusian blood. The mares in this road are of Andalusian blood, almost pure. A sister to my father, the lady Broquel, came with her husband to this country. She brought ten mares and a stallion of the purest blood. A few times through the years she sent for fresh blood from the Ranch of the Tree. She cared, but she is old and lives in San Antonio now; and her grandson does not care. He is the young Collin."

He went on to say that the young Collin's parents were deceased. There were other heirs, but none who were interested in the ranch. And the grandmother knew little of what went on. My friend said that when he saw the Shield mares were going to be disposed of, scattered to the winds, that he decided a horseman should have them. This would prevent their going to the open market to be thrown just wherever they might land. He told me all this in a sad and lonely voice, glancing at me occasionally, but for the most part he looked at the mares or across the dry river into the desert regions of Mexico.

He explained to me about the crossing he wanted to use to go into Mexico. My road that turned north was just about two or three miles farther up. I knew the general lay of the country pretty well; and I knew the road he was explaining to me well enough that when I got on it I could handle the mares and go on by myself. They were nice to handle, and they had been no real trouble since we got them off that home range that they had been taught to get away in.

I had never seen any pure-blooded Andalusians, and I had begun to look at these mares closely. He told me that the Andalusian horse was the purest of Spanish blood, and that this strain was as old a tribe as the Arabs or the Turks or any of the other old tribes of horses. The Andalusians had been bred in the mountains for bone and muscle, substance and endurance, and all the other things it takes to make a fine horse. Much attention had been given to the selection of individuals with good dispositions. All of this showed strongly in the mares in front of us.

We were about to reach the point where he wanted to turn off and go down and cross the Rio Grande into Mexico. I said, "You haven't said which mares you want."

He said, "The brand you thought was blotched, it is the Shield brand over the Tree on the last mares that left our ranch. It would be to my liking—and I should be forever grateful—if I could have two of the Shield mares which have been branded over the Tree. I would take them back to the land of my father, who yet lives, that he may see we still have some of the old and true blood."

"I think you'll be cheatin' yourself in age. These are the oldest mares here."

He said, "Yes, they will be twenty-four years old. It has been that long since they were born, although they were sent to this country as yearling fillies. Their purity of blood is beyond doubt. They will be all I shall ask of you."

I told him to cut them out and put halters on them to lead them away. I rode up in front and rode around the mares and stopped them. There was a little bit of grazing, and they stopped and picked on what they could find. I realized

then that there were four of the Tree mares that had the
blotched brand where the Shield had been branded over.
These mares were old. They wouldn't mean as much to me
as they would to him; so when we drove the mares on past
the corner where he was going to turn off, and as he turned
back to lead his two mares off and these other two old mares
were watching them leave, I just rode up and put back these
two old mares that had chummed in the pasture with the
two he was taking.

He crossed into old Mexico with the four Tree mares. And
I went up the road with twenty-four of the purest Andalusian
mares in the New World.

I found water about two o'clock that afternoon where a
creek crossed the road. My mares filled up, rested, and I
drove on up the road. With a bunch of loose horses on an
open road, you go to hunting a place to spend the night with
them along about midafternoon. About two hours before
sundown, I found a set of working pens by the side of the
road. They were inside a ranch pasture with a water trough
and a windmill. There was no grass in the pasture, there was
no grass in the pens; but it was a place to hold them overnight. They had found a small amount of grazing along
during the day.

I opened the gates and set them where the horses would
go into these corrals. Then I rode on past the horses and
turned them back and put them in these pens. It was a good
deal before dark, and it would give me time to make a little
camp, fix myself some supper, and clean my saddle horse
off and wash his back. I'd noticed that there were two or
three of these mares that had saddle marks on them. I had
about decided that the next day I would ride a mare and let
my saddle horse rest. In this extra time, I could catch one
or two or three of them, maybe saddle them up and see
about their mouths, and see which one I thought might do to
ride.

I picked out a blood-bay mare with black feet and legs,

black mane and tail—about an eight-year-old that had cinch marks on her. I had run her around in the corral a little bit and kinda gotten her uncorked, and I knew she was going to be all right. Nobody came by my camp to see who I was or visit or anything. It was a lonesome spot, but that didn't bother me much.

I turned my horses in the road early next morning and started the day's drive. There were a few cars in the road that day, not many, and I hadn't passed but one ranch head-quarters. It was set way off from the side of the road, so I didn't go by there. But about the middle of the afternoon, a car overtook me. Driving this car was a lady dressed in white—not exactly a nurse's uniform, but later I saw she had a nurse's pin on. Sitting in front with her was a cowboy of average make and age, clean-shaven and nice looking, but strictly a man of the range. And in the back seat was an old white-headed lady. She was very frail and very old, but at a glance you could tell that she was a very refined person.

They drove through very slowly, as if they were counting these mares, and the elderly lady raised up and sat on the edge of the back seat and looked out the door. This was a fine, old automobile and beautifully kept. It seemed as if the old lady was having it driven slowly while she looked at every mare. They drove on past about a mile and turned the car around. They were facing the horses as I drove them down the little slope in a walk—and the man got out of the car and walked around and went to stopping my horses as I got up close to the car. He motioned for me to ride around the mares and up to the car, and I could see that the old lady was wanting to talk to me.

She didn't waste any time in telling me she was the grand-mother of the young Collin from whom I had bought my mares. She told me, "I live in San Antonio because I am too old to look after the ranch, but I know that the Shield Ranch must have mares to raise saddle horses from, and I just hope some of the other members of the family will learn this before it is too late. This may be my last chance to impress this fact upon them. Would you consider selling me these Shield mares?" She went on to say, "I have counted the mares. I am not sure how many there should be, but I do know there still should be some mares with the Tree branded on them. I do not see any mares of the Tree. What has happened to them?"

I didn't really know how plain to talk to this fine old lady. I hesitated telling her what happened to the mares with the Tree. I told her that I wanted to keep most of the mares, that I was young and had a small ranch, and I wanted to always have good horses. Now that I had some Shield mares, I didn't take well to the thought of disposing of them—even before I got home.

She said that she knew I bought the mares to keep and that I, as a horseman, was entitled to keep some mares—or make a profit—or both—but that she was old, profit didn't matter a great deal to her, but she hated to lose the last of the mares. Again she asked, "Did you see the mares with the Tree? The Shield is branded over the Tree."

I told her that I was sympathetic with her situation, but that if I hoped to have good horses all my life I needed most of these mares, and that there were only twenty-four left in the band.

She quickly caught the word *left*. She said, "You must have had the Tree mares. Señor Gonzales at the mercantile store called me in San Antonio and said twenty-eight mares stayed overnight in the corrals at his store. He also told me of a white-haired horseman who was riding with you. He is gone—and the four mares of the Tree."

I could tell that this old lady was pretty sharp, knew what she was talking about, and was a great old ranchwoman that time had overtaken. I finally told her that Don Ricardo Olivorez had helped me get the Shield mares out of the pasture and into the road, and for his services he had taken the four mares of the Tree. He was riding a horse branded with the Tree, and he had crossed over into Mexico the day before about ten or eleven o'clock in the morning.

She leaned back against the back seat of the car and sighed deeply. She closed her eyes, her lips moved silently, and I saw her make the sign of the cross. I was standing in the doorway of the car, and I just stood there as respectfully as I could until she finally opened her eyes and looked back at me. She looked for some time, and then she said, "Young man, sell me the mares."

I said, "I'll sell you half of them—which would be twelve —and that would leave me twelve."

She said, "I am prepared to pay for them." She hadn't yet asked the price, but she told the cowboy to open the trunk and get his saddle and riggin' out—which he immediately began to do.

I insisted that I keep the three mares with the saddle marks on them, and from the rest they could take their half. The mares were scattered up and down the fenceline, grazing in the bar ditch of the road on what little grass they could find. She made no comment, except, "There could be but little difference in the mares of the Shield." So I told her we would just walk down the road and cut off the twelve that were nearest on the way back to the Shield Ranch.

She said, "And how much money shall I pay you?"

I said, "Seven hundred and fifty dollars. That is the amount I gave for all of them. I'll have my twelve clear, other than the trip and expenses."

The nurse in the front seat opened a large handbag and took out my money in large bills. The old lady scooted comfortably in the back seat and thanked me very much. She neither mentioned that the mares were high nor cheap, nor that she cared one way or another. The only thing she seemed to be interested in was that she had recovered twelve mares of the Shield to send back to the ranch. Whether she paid me a profit or not was of no concern to her.

I consented to let the cowboy have one of the mares that

had saddle marks on her. He saddled one up and walked her around a few minutes and stepped on her. Her manners were nice, just like the one I was riding. The old lady thanked me another time or two and drove on off toward the Ranch of the Shield.

I started on up the road into the foothills of the live oak country with my twelve Andalusian mares, my saddle horse, all my money back, and the possibility and probability that I would be mounted on good horses as long as I lived.

WATERMELON HAULER'S MULE

It was late summer and in the cool of the afternoon the air was almost fallish. I was standin' in front of the wagonyard, watchin' the empty watermelon wagons and a few cotton wagons that had come in loaded that morning go down the road leavin' town. A watermelon farmer drove up by the side of the fence and stopped his team, then started up toward the John Hart Grocery Store. I suppose he wanted to get some grub to take home with him. He was dressed in overalls and country straw hat, a blue faded shirt and tennis shoes, and had a dip of snuff that had seeped out a little on his whiskers. He didn't look like one of nature's brightest individuals as he shuffled off up the sandy street into the store.

I didn't walk out to his wagon, but stood there lookin' at his team. They were badly mismatched for size, color, breed, and sex. One was a big, stout, roughly finished brown horse, workin' on the left; the other was a little bitty, fat, smooth sorrel mare mule, working on the right, which is just the backwards way of hitchin' up two work animals of different size. The biggest and heaviest one ought to be on the right because there is a little more pull on the horse workin' nearest the ditch and on the slope of a country road. I liked the looks of this little sorrel mule. I noticed that her feet and legs were good and sound, and she was fat, which always helps the looks of any horse or mule.

It was nearly dusk when this watermelon cropper came shufflin' back down that sandy road with an apple box full of groceries. I smiled and raised my voice and said, "Neighbor, why don't you have a horse trade with me. I've got something to match the little mule or to match the big horse, whichever one you'd like to trade off."

He kinda grinned, set his groceries over in the wagon, and said he shore wished he had a mate to that nice big horse. Before he said too much, he caught himself and began to explain to me what a good work mule the sorrel mare mule was and how proud he was of her, but he said he didn't think she looked good hitched up by that great big horse. I agreed with him right off because I'd rather have the mule than the horse to resell, so we walked back toward the back side of the wagonyard to my tradin' pen.

I had two or three horses that any one of them would match his big horse. He looked at 'em and felt of 'em and walked around 'em and he finally picked out a big, fat, honest nine-year-old brown horse that was a real good match for the horse he had. We talked on about the horse and the mule and I took a rope and put it around the horse's neck and led him back up toward the wagon, because I wanted him to see that he would look good next to his big horse.

It was nearly dark and I looked into the mule's mouth and could tell she was about an eight-year-old; there wasn't much difference between her age and my horse's age. Of course, I made him a pretty good speech about a big fat horse being worth more than a little bitty mule, most of which wasn't necessarily so, but I didn't think he'd know the difference. I asked him $20 boot, and he said watermelons hadn't been sellin' that good but he believed he'd give $10 boot just because that brown horse would look better than that little bitty sorrel mare mule did. It didn't take me too long to decide that would be plenty boot and that we'd just have a horse trade.

We unhitched his little mule and took her harness off, and 'course we had to let out the traces and the backband and the bellyband and all that kind of stuff to get his harness to fit this big horse. By this time it was just about dark. He picked up the lead rope that was on the mule and said, "I'll lead the mule down and put her in the lot for you while you kinds adjest the bridle on that horse's head."

I knew this horse was pretty cold-shouldered and just might not want to work off too good, even to an empty wagon. And somethin' he hadn't bothered to ask me was "if'n my horse would work."

There is a stay chain on a wagon on each side that hooks

to the front axle and then there's a hook on the doubletree, and by adjustin' the length of the stay chain, you can be sure that each of your team is gettin' the proper pull on his end of the doubletree. While this old, kinda dumb snuff-dipper was gone to put my mule in the lot, I reached down and shortened the stay chain on the horse he already had hooked to be sure that when they started off, he'd move the load without this tradin' horse that I was lettin' him have havin' to pull any weight.

He came back in a minute and I helped him hook up the horse. He paid me the $10 in cash and stepped up in the spring seat and thanked me. He shook the lines and clucked to his team, and, sure enough, his horse moved the wagon and they drove off pretty as you please in the dark.

Next morning I went down to my trade lot about sunup and that sorrel mare mule had her head stickin' over the fence facing the sunrise, and she sure didn't look too good with my horses either 'cause she was plumb blind!

GITTIN'
EVEN

The horse and mule market had opened up in the fall real good and had gotten better as the season went on. I had several orders for mares with weanling-age colts by their sides, and I also wanted some well-bred usin'-type mares to turn in my own pasture. It was a fact that you could get mares and colts cheaper if you bought them together than you could if you bought them separate and a trader always figured that if he sold the colts he would nearly clear the mares— or that if he sold the mares he would nearly clear the colts—so in horse tradin' times, to a trader mares and colts were good property.

I wanted to try to buy a pretty big bunch of these pairs, so I decided to go out West where horses ran in bunches and people talked in bigger figures. I drove into San Angelo and sat around the hotel lobby nearly all day visitin' and askin' about mares and colts, and finally an old boy heard what I was huntin' for and came over and struck up a conversation. He told me that Old Man Garner on the Pecos River at Girvin Switch had lots of mares and colts. He said he thought it was the custom to let a man pick what he wanted to buy since pickin' wouldn't hurt Old Man

Garner because he had so many horses; and a fellow might shape up a pretty nice set of young mares with breedy colts sired by thoroughbred studs.

Well, I took in all this conversation and told him that I had about half changed my mind and thought I might go back without any mares. He said, "That's your privilege, but if you want some good ones, don't pass up seein' Old Man Garner's horses."

I didn't much more than let him get out of sight before I mounted my six-cylinder Buick and started out to see Old Man Garner. It was late afternoon and about a hundred-mile trip, so I drove to Rankin and spent the night. Next morning I wasn't more than twenty-five or thirty miles from Garner's headquarters on the Pecos River. I got there by daylight and stepped up on the porch, cleared my throat, and hollered hello. This was strictly an old horse ranch and several riders were in the kitchen eatin' a ranch breakfast. The cook came to the door hollerin', "Come in," and said, "Go on back to the kitchen. Breakfast is ready."

Old Man Garner was settin' at the head of the table and I introduced myself. He didn't bother to get up—he just wiped the egg out of his beard and said, "Sit down and have some breakfast."

During grub, coffee, and conversation, I got it over to the old man what my mission was. He said he was always glad to see a horse buyer and it didn't make any difference what age, size, or color horses I wanted, he had plenty for me to cut 'em from. He explained to me that I couldn't see horses on this ranch in an automobile and that these horses had moved into the breaks along the river since cold weather and he could get up a bunch of mares and colts that day and I could come back tomorrow to see 'em. There was a little comment around the table among the horse wranglers that it wouldn't be no trouble to get a bunch close into headquarters by dark.

I thought this was a good arrangement. I was gonna get

to see all the mares and colts in one place that I had money to buy and it would save a lot of drivin' and huntin' for just a few at a time. I circled around the country a little the rest of the day and spent the night at Ozona.

I was back at Garner's about ten o'clock the next morning. He had about two hundred and fifty head of mares with colts and a dozen or so studs in a great big corral. His mares showed to have a lot of thoroughbred even though they were range mares that had never been broke and showed no signs of good care or attention. You could tell that they hadn't been run or worked too much to get them in to that small pasture, and even though it was dead of winter, their hair wasn't very long and didn't show any signs of sweat from runnin'.

Old Man Garner said these horses weren't too used to people afoot or ahorseback, but if I would get on one of their saddle horses we could ease around through 'em and I could pick out what I wanted to buy and he would see if he could stand to sell 'em. When you are buying this kind of mare you are not going to have a chance to mouth them and look at their teeth for age, so you try to pick ones with good, bright, young-lookin' heads and the kind of body and legs that it takes to raise good colts.

I told the old man that I could buy about ninety head of these mares with the colts throwed in, which was a common way of tradin' in those days. He thought they ought to be worth about $50 for mare and colt, but I had a big difference of opinion about that and we finally traded for me to give $35 a head for the mare with the colt throwed in.

In a pasture over the fence from these horses I noticed some dry mares that were fat and some of 'em were stiff from being run. Garner told me that they had been cut away from the mares with colts. I also noticed a few mares in another pasture with colts on 'em and their colts were either lyin' down or standin' propped up against their mammies; these were the smallest colts, and the old man told me he thought I wouldn't be interested in those. This made good sense and I didn't question it further.

After agreein' on the price, we were down to the matter of me pickin' ninety mares with colts out of the two hundred and fifty pairs. These were light-boned breedy mares that had big colts on them. After dinner we worked ninety pairs out of that big corral into a smaller one and everybody kept cautionin' me not to get 'em hot, to work 'em easy and not to run 'em. All kinds of cautionin' was goin' on, which wasn't customary on an old Pecos River ranch where colts were raised from unbroke mares.

Occasionally I would see a mare stumble and nearly go to her knees and I just thought that was because her feet were long or she might be a little weak from suckin' a colt. When we had 'em cut off and shaped up like I wanted 'em, it seemed to me that some of these colts were a bit listless. I noticed one standin' kind of spraddle-legged and backed up against the fence, but when I walked by and jiggered at him, he jumped out; apparently there was nothin' wrong with him.

I had to go to Fort Stockton to order cars to be spotted by the railroad at the shippin' pens next day and Old Man Garner said that they would turn the mares out and drive 'em down to the stock pens late that afternoon and that they would haul 'em enough alfalfa hay to last during the night. I bought one saddle horse from him for $50 to be left at the stock pens with the mares, which made me pay him an even $3,200. He was real anxious to drive the mares down that afternoon, furnish 'em hay for the night, and load 'em the next morning on the train. He told me that if I wanted to I could go on back to Fort Worth and he would take care of the whole deal.

I thought he seemed a little anxious to get rid of me, but, on the other hand, a trader way off from home would like to have a head start on beatin' the train back so he can be there to see his horses unloaded. So I decided to take him up on his proposition. Him and his horse wranglers kept assurin' me that I wouldn't have anything to worry about—they would take care of them just as good as I would and for me to head on back, I might even find some more horses to buy.

At Fort Stockton I ordered three forty-foot cars for my ninety mares with colts. The railroad rarely had forty-foot cars and if you ordered them and they didn't have them, they had to furnish you two thirty-sixes at the price of one forty-foot. A thirty-six-foot car would hold from twenty-four to as many as thirty light-boned range-type horses or about twenty to twenty-four mares with colts would be all that you could possibly load in a thirty-six-foot car. By ordering forty-foot cars I was gamblin' that they wouldn't have 'em and I was figurin' that I would put fifteen mares and fifteen colts in each of the six thirty-six-foot cars, which would give the horses plenty of room for a long shipment.

Sure enough, they didn't have any forty-foot cars and the railroad agent told me they would give me six thirty-six-foot cars instead. I headed on back to Fort Worth and left the rest of the horse deal for Old Man Garner to complete according to our agreement.

I got into Fort Worth the next morning but didn't go around to the stockyard or horse and mule barns until about middle of the next day when I began to look for my horses to come in. The train backed the car into Ross Bros. Horse and Mule Market just a little after dark and started unloadin' 'em. Of course, these horses had had plenty of room—some had lain down in the cars. There were none crippled or injured from the haul, but there were sixteen dead mares and twenty-one dead colts in the six cars! The ones still alive were all shakin' and jerkin' and staggerin' when they walked, but they went to the troughs and drank water and began to nibble on the prairie hay in the hayrack. There was plenty of grain, oats, and corn mixed in the feed trough, but none of these range mares or colts knew how to eat grain. They were badly drawn, with listless eyes and poor appetites, and all of 'em staggered from a little to a whole lot when they tried to move.

I called the barn veterinarian. He came down and looked and felt and took temperatures. None of 'em showed any sign of known disease and he confessed that he had no idea what was the matter with 'em or what would help 'em, and for the little good that he had done, he guessed he'd let me off for $25. The loss of so many horses and the cost of the vet bill and the fact that I had my tradin' money tied up in a bunch of sick horses I couldn't sell was makin' me wobble and stagger a little too.

The railroad agent sent a man down the next morning and we made out a claim for the twenty-one colts and sixteen mares. Wad Ross had me leave these mares and colts in the back of the barn next to the railroad where as few people as possible would see 'em, and he was scared that they had some kind of disease that would spread through the barn. I sat around in the feed troughs and watched these horses all day without the slightest idea of what was the matter with 'em or what to do for 'em. We had the stockyards dead wagon pick up from one to five head every morning for a week. And, then, the rest of them began to fill up and be snorty like range horses are supposed to be.

I had lost a total of forty colts and thirty-two mares, leaving me fifty-eight mares and fifty colts to try to get my money out of, and I still didn't know nor had I found anybody that knew what was the matter with this bunch of horses. After they had begun to do good, I started showin' them to people and gettin' ready to sell them at auction because I didn't want to sell 'em to any of my customers and sure didn't want to take 'em to my pasture.

I was sittin' in the dining room of the old Stockyards Hotel and Port Daggett came in, shook hands, and sat down by me. We went to talkin' about our business. I knew he had done lots of business west of the Pecos River and I opened up to him a little and said, "Port, do you know Old Man Garner at Girvin?"

He said, "Yeah, he's got that old horse ranch down there where all that alkali weed is. Half of his horses die every winter."

"What kind of weed?" I asked.

"Alkali weed. They don't eat it until after frost, and the mares that suck colts pass it through the milk and kill the colts, but it don't hurt the mares lots of times.

"If you don't move 'em or run 'em and leave 'em alone when the grass comes green in the spring, they git it out of their system. But it will sure kill 'em if you handle 'em."

I didn't let on. I just said, "Well, if a man's gonna buy any horses, he'd better wait until spring."

He said, "That's for sure, but the old man's got well-bred horses and he always sells 'em cheap enough, and if you was aimin' to get any of 'em, just wait until the alkali weed's out of 'em and buy 'em in the spring."

Someone hollered at Port and he slapped me on the back as he left with a bunch of fellows, never realizing he had just dropped the boom on me.

After another week's feed bill, these mares and colts showed no signs of anything being wrong with 'em and I ran 'em through the auction. In spite of all the dead ones, I had bought 'em so cheap that they really didn't hurt me as bad as it had looked like they would at times. However, I was about $700 the loser and a very little bit wiser, but when you get your hook hung on something like that the only way you can get back to makin' money is to get loose from it so you can go back to the brush and hunt for more stock. So after these five or six weeks of experience and losin' money, I thought I would change directions and head into South Texas.

I was at the old Gunter Hotel in San Antonio one night visitin' around the lobby with stockmen I knew when Major Atkins from the government remount service walked up and began to talk about seven stallions that they had taken back from ranchers because all seven of these stallions had proved to be sterile and the ranchers had a bunch of barren mares for that year that the government had assigned them these studs.

Next morning I went out to Charlie Krinskey's Mule Barn and heard him tell some other fellows that Old Man Garner had called him the night before and said he was comin' to San Antonio to buy some studs, preferably thoroughbreds, and if any of the boys listenin' had any thoroughbred studs, tomorrow would be the day to have them at the sale. I went back to the hotel and was sittin' in the lobby wonderin' what to do next when I saw Major Atkins come in the front door. He walked up to my chair and I got up and shook hands with him and visited for a few minutes. He started to leave and had stepped off a step or two, then turned back and asked as though it was an afterthought, "Ben, what would you do with some thoroughbred sterile studs?"

I said, "I've never found a very ready market for that kind of a stud. What would the salvage price be on 'em?"

"Twenty-five dollars a head if you would move 'em in the next few days."

I said, "I can't see that there would be any point in takin' up much of mine and your time to go see a bunch of sterile studs. I'll either castrate 'em for usin' horses or cut their throats if I want to, so I'll just give you a check for 'em."

Well, we had to go up to his room and draw up one of them damn long government forms of some kind for me to sign before he could take my check, and he told me he would drive out with me to show me where the horses were when I got ready to move 'em.

I said, "That'll be in about thirty minutes."

I called Pat Bridges that we would be by in a few minutes and told him to pick up a saddle and riggin' because I wanted him to bring some horses to town. Pat was an old brokedown cowboy that made a livin' movin' horses around the stockyards for people. The Major and I picked him up in the Major's car and drove about four miles south of town, where these stallions were in a government barn.

Pat checked them out and picked the one that had the fewest blemishes and cuts on him and might ride the best. There was a lot of fightin' and bitin' and kickin' in these studs, but Pat had plenty of halters to put on 'em and let 'em drag the ropes to where he could herd 'em. He took a bullwhip down off his saddle where he could ride into 'em and break up fights. I helped him get 'em in the road and start 'em to the stockyards, which was between there and town. I guess the fightin' and bitin' and playin' didn't last long, 'cause I was at the barn when he came in with 'em. We put them in separate stalls and they didn't show to have skinned each other up very much.

I went into the office and consigned seven registered thoroughbred studs and left their registration papers at the office. Next morning I was out early to see about my high-bred stock and saw Old Man Garner at a distance across the barn lookin' at some other horses. I went by the office and told 'em to mail me my check when my horses were sold—I had somewhere else to go. By the middle of the week, I made it back home and went by the post office and picked up a check for $925 and noticed that the buyer on all seven head was marked GARNER.

WATER TREATMENT
TREATMENT
AND THE
SORE-TAILED
BRONC

It was late fall and the leaves had turned the many hues that nature provides to bring the close to a green season and to warn animal life that harder days are yet to come. I had had a rough summer and had ridden my best horses on longer and harder rides than they should have had to stand, so I pulled the shoes off Beauty and turned her in a pasture to get some rest before the cold weather set in. Of course, she knew that when it got cold I would bring her back to the barn for feed, and I know she was havin' a good time.

I didn't have a whole lot of ridin' to do and I had been usin' some plain and green kind of tradin' horses. Coming up the road late one afternoon near Springtown, I saw a pen full of horses near the road and a couple of fellows ropin' some out of the bunch. I reined by the corral fence and set on this not too good a horse I was ridin' and watched for a few minutes.

We had our howdie. One of these boys was named Tom Young and he asked, "Ben, which one of these horses do you want to trade for that one you're ridin'?"

I said, "What's the matter with that good-lookin' red roan?"

Well, Tom set in to tell me that he was a good saddle horse, gentle to ride, and had been restin' all summer, and I sure had topped his bunch at a glance. I said, "That's the speech you had ready for whoever asked about him, but you misunderstood me. I asked what all's the matter with him?"

He said, "I'm tellin' you the truth. He's been runnin' out all summer. We'll catch and saddle him and he'll never hump up, offer to buck, or do anything wrong."

Tom dropped a rope on the roan's neck and I

looked in his mouth and saw that he was an honest eight-year-old. His legs were clean and his body was well balanced and he lacked about two inches being as tall as the bay horse I was ridin', which would suit me since, being short-legged, it would make it easier for me to get on.

We put my saddle on him and, sure enough, he didn't seem to have any mean in him. There was nothin' much wrong with the horse I was ridin' except that his back was a little too long, his girth a little too shallow, and his legs a little too crooked, so I finally agreed to give him and $20 boot in trade for the red roan.

By the time I got to Veal Station, the red roan had settled down; he was a real good travelin' horse, had a fast runnin' walk and a nice way of carryin' himself, and I just thought to myself, a man can still make a good trade every now and then.

I rode in home about ten o'clock that night. This old pony was pretty soft and hadn't been used, and when I turned him loose in the corral, he had worked up a big sweat and was sure enough tired. He rolled and wallered in the dirt and lay there a good while before he got up to come eat. It was a moonlight night, and although the weather had gotten pretty nippy, I stood around and watched him until he started eatin', thinkin' I might have rode him too hard.

I saddled him early the next morning and started south to the Brazos River to look at five head of horses near the Dennis Schoolhouse that I had promised a man I would see. I never had had an occasion to tie this red roan horse and I hadn't been off of him but a few times since the day before. The five head of horses at Dennis were from the old Hubbard stock and were known to be of fox-trottin' blood. They were all pretty big horses—fifteen hands and over—four to six years old, and none of them broke. This wasn't too uncommon since we rarely broke a horse until he was big and stout enough to carry a man at least half a day. Breakin' two-year-olds was unheard of and we broke very few threes.

Of course, breakin' four- and five-year-old horses was harder work and harder ridin', but you had a heap more under you by the time you got 'em broke and shod and on hard feed.

A cotton farmer who was sort of a coward about horses owned these particular horses and they weren't much trouble to buy. In the trade he agreed to keep them in the lot for me for two or three days while I rode on down the country and I would pick them up on the way back. About noon that same day I had reached the Brazos and had turned down a little road that followed the river. About a mile from the Dennis Bridge I saw a little glade, and I thought it would be a good place to stop and feed my horse and fix myself some dinner.

The weather wasn't real cold and I was travelin' light—I had two blankets rolled up in my slicker behind my saddle and in the middle of that roll I had enough meat and bread for a couple of days' ride. I slipped the bridle off this good roan horse that I had really begun to like, put my lariat rope on him, and tied him to a tree. I poured about a gallon of oats on a pile of fresh fallen leaves at the base of the tree so that he could pretty well eat without gettin' any dirt in his feed.

I built a little fire and took out a big pocketknife and was slicing some meat when I heard a commotion—this good red roan horse was about to show off. He was one of those horses that didn't like to be tied. He was groanin' and settin' back with all he had, tryin' to break that good four-strand manilla lariat rope. I squalled at him and walked over to him, but that just made him worse. I had fixed the rope so that it wouldn't choke him and he was fast peelin' his head and neck with that hard rope. Now I knew from some of the other dark patches of hair around over his head that he had broke more bridles than he was worth. It just so happened that I had taken the bridle off of him and had taken the bits out of his mouth so he could eat.

There's nothin' more aggravatin' to a man ahorseback

than to have a horse he can't tie with a bridle rein. The roan would take a bite or two of feed and then all of a sudden fall back with all his weight on that rope. I went back to my fire and finished my dinner and by this time he had already pulled against the tree six or seven times and had his head and neck pretty well skinned up. I pitched my saddle over at about the right angle and fixed my blanket and thought I would take a little afternoon nap, but I couldn't get to sleep for listenin' to him groan, pull, and fight. To think that I saw those different colors of hair around on his head and neck and didn't get the message when I was tradin' for him! Sure enough, he had been restin' all summer—to heal up and peel off all the scabs from the last time he had been tied.

His hindquarters weren't more than twenty feet from the bank of the river and it was about half full. I was rollin' my grub back into my blanket and slicker and tying them on my saddle when he groaned and fell back again. I made a dash at him and cut the rope. He fell end over end off the bank of the river on his back and made about a twenty-foot splash. I watched the water rush in and cover up his nose; he nearly sank before he came up blowin' water out of his nose and tryin' to swim. I walked along the bank and watched him when he came out of the river on a sand bar about a mile from where he had fallen in. It was no trouble to walk up to and catch the end of the rope because he was tryin' hard to get a few gallons of water blown out of his lungs. I let him stand there spraddle-legged and cough and wheeze until he finally caught his breath. Then I led him back to where my saddle and riggin' was and I thought to myself, I might have given him the cure on that rarin' back.

For the next two or three days everybody that saw him who knew anything about a horse had to hurrah me a little about gettin' a spoiled horse traded to me. By the time I got back to where I had bought the five head of horses, the water treatment caused the roan to develop an awful case of distemper. He was blowin' his nose and heavin' for breath and wasn't gettin' me over very much country. The unbroke horses that I turned in the road to drive to town were gentle to pen and handle and be around but just never had been rode.

About middle of the afternoon, my consumptive red roan horse had about given out. I eased up alongside of a four-year-old light chestnut horse in my bunch and dropped a rope on him. He had been caught before and didn't put up too much of a struggle and I managed to get his back foot tied up to a shoulder and get my saddle and riggin' on him in the middle of the road. He was a big horse and I knew that if he bucked I might not be able to ride him and if he tried to run, I would probably lose the rest of them, so I had the bright idea that my settin'-back horse might be real useful.

I put a rope halter on all those skinned, sore places on his head and led him up close to the bronc horse. I doubled the loose hair on the bronc horse's tail back up and tied a knot in it and then I double half-hitched this roan horse's halter rope into the bronc's tail. It was a public road but there wasn't none of the public comin' along to help me about this time, so I pushed the bronc around until I got him down in the ditch to where I could step on him real quick. Then I untied his back foot from the saddle horn and let it down. By now he was pretty disturbed and the other horses were just grazin' along up the road. When he felt he had all four feet on the ground, he fully intended to come undone. He bawled and jumped into the air, and when he did I squalled and waved my hat back at my red roan horse and he set back and held the bronc on the ground.

I wasn't makin' much time because the roan didn't come up and give my bronc any slack often enough and we were travelin' pretty bad. The bronc couldn't very well turn around because when he did I would squall at the roan and he would set back and pull him to the ground. After an hour or so of this cowboy'n', the roan began to lead pretty good so that I could set the bronc along and make him go forward and slap him on the jaw with my hand to make him go the direction I wanted. Along about mid-evening we caught up with the other horses on the road in front of us. All of this activity had kept a pretty constant rub on those skinned places on the red roan's head.

There was a set of open corrals on a ranch close to the road and I made it there about dark and unrigged my horses and made out my pallet. After a pretty good supper of meat and bread, I didn't have any trouble dozin' off in that crisp fall air. I had let the roan horse wear the halter all night; in case he wanted to feel some pain, he could step on the rope. By now those sore places on his head had dried and chaffed up pretty bad, so he was gettin' the full benefit of the damage done by his own bad disposition.

Next morning I rigged up halters with drag ropes and caught the broncs while I had them in a good pen. When I turned them out about sunup with my sore-headed horse tied to my sore-tailed bronc, I knew that they weren't goin' to be too much trouble to drive. I loose-herded these horses into the wagonward a little after dinnertime. I was ridin' a green bronc and I was hopin' I had broke the roan from some bad habits. I knew that the roan was gentle and that he wouldn't go "broncy" if I let him rest, so I turned him in the pasture with Beauty for the skinned places on his head and neck to heal up and peel off.

In about a month I rode him up by the drugstore and stepped off but didn't tie him. I left his rein on the ground, which cowboys refer to as "ground tied." Monty Thomas came along and recognized the horse. He had owned him sometime back and liked him so well that he would never have traded him off except for his bad habit. He very sneakingly reached down, picked up the reins and tied them to the post, and then walked up to the corner of the building facing the square, where he could watch the roan break loose.

I was gone twenty or thirty minutes and I came back around the corner, spoke to Monty, and walked on and saw that my horse was tied to the post and he hadn't tried to break loose. Monty hollered, "Wait a minute. I used to own that horse and would still own him if it hadn't been for a bad habit or two that he had. I want to know how you broke him from settin' back on the rein and tearin' up the bridle."

I said, "Monty, I don't know what you're talkin' about. As far as I know, this horse hasn't got a bad habit in the world."

He walked around him and looked at the roan carefully and said, "He's the same horse."

Before night, Tom Young came to the wagonyard and said that Monty had told him that he had tied the horse and he didn't offer to set back. I said, "Well, I guess you boys just never held your mouth right or had poor judgment or bad riggin' because I don't have a nicer horse to ride than this one."

Tom asked, "How did you break him?"

"He was broke when I got him. You told me that and how gentle he was," I said, just like I didn't know what he was talkin' about.

He said, "I'll give you the horse back that you traded to me and $50 boot for him."

"Tom," I said, "I rarely if ever trade a horse off that I want back, but I'll take $200 for the roan."

"Why, Ben, you know there ain't no horse worth $200!"

And, I knew that was really the truth according to the times. He said, "I want to ride him. There couldn't be two horses look that much alike and I know how he ought to feel under me."

I told him to help himself. He rode off down toward the feed mill and was gone a long time. The reason he was gone so long was that he had ridden down there and tied him and got off of him and he told me that he even slapped him in the face with his hat and he couldn't get him to set back, but he did know it was the same horse.

I said, "You ought not to slap a nice horse in the face with your hat. You might teach him bad habits."

We had lots of conversation and ate supper together and I never let on that I knew anything had ever been wrong with the horse. The next morning before I left town, Tom came by the wagonyard and, finally, after an awful lot of palaver, gave me $165 for the red roan horse and nobody until now ever knew about the water treatment and the sore-tailed bronc.

CINDY

One hot July afternoon I was sittin' in one of the town drugstores with Dr. Chandler, a good old-fashioned family doctor with lots of common sense who always had his patients' welfare at heart, when Cindy, a crippled little girl about eight years old, came into the drugstore on crutches to get an ice-cream cone. Dr. Chandler had something nice to say to Cindy, the same as he did to everybody else, and as she left the store, the old doctor straightened the little black bowtie that was around his stiff winged-point white collar and shook his head and said, "What a shame."

I was a rough young cowboy and wasn't too much worried about the ills of the world and so I said, "What do you mean, 'What a shame'?"

Without being malicious, Dr. Chandler said that if Cindy hadn't been so well cared for after her rheumatic fever that her feet would not have drawn the way they had. Her family was a little too well fixed and had taken too much care of her. Well, I knew this to be true because they had hired private teachers so she wouldn't have to go to school on crippled feet and there was always domestic help around the house to wait on Cindy. The doctor continued and said that if there was some way she could be made to take exercise, her feet might be saved even this late. In a very idle, lighthearted way I said, "I have a mare with feet crippled like her. If you find out how, we'll save 'em both."

The old doctor just shook his head and said, "Ben, you'll never do."

Our backyard was just across the alley from Cindy's and I had a little horse pasture running from the barn down to the creek where I kept an extra horse or two besides the one I would be riding. The pony I had mentioned to Dr. Chandler was a little red roan, bald-faced, stocking-legged Indian pony a little larger than a Shetland, but not horse size, that had been foundered from too much feed.

Ponies are inclined to be more subject to founder from eating too much rich protein feed than big horses, and this little mare that I had named Pocahontas had foundered several times. Founder is a supersaturation of protein that settles around the joints of the legs of horses and causes the feet to fever, and as the foot grows out it wrinkles and contracts at the heel unless the horse is kept shod and the hooves are treated to keep them soft.

Well, this little mare wasn't exactly worthless because I sometimes would turn her into a pasture to use as a decoy for wilder horses to take up with and make them easier to drive or get out of the pasture. And, too, Pocahontas had been a good baby sitter with colts when they were weaned off of their mother. I could put them with Pocahontas and she seemed to keep them from getting in the fence and trying to get back to their mothers.

I had brought Pocahontas into town and was keeping her in the small pasture and her feet were in extremely bad shape because she had run out all winter and spring and I had not cut the extra growth off that was turning the ends of her hooves up. They had grown out until her front feet stuck up a little at the toes and she was walking on the outside of her foot and her heel about like little Cindy. I began thinking that if I got Pocahontas and little Cindy together, they might help each other, so I put the little mare in the corral right behind Cindy's house and cut the water off from the water trough in the corral.

I didn't see what went on that day, but sometime during the afternoon Cindy was out in her backyard where she could hold on to an ornamental iron fence and walk and Pocahontas nickered at her. Cindy held on to the iron fence and made her way back to the alley between the corral that Pocahontas was in and the iron fence of her backyard. When I rode in late that afternoon Cindy came down that iron fence pretty fast and said in a straight forward manner, "That sweet little horse has been nickerin' all afternoon, and I think it's because she doesn't have any water."

I said, "Well, Miss Cindy, I have to lead Pocahontas."

She laughed real quick and thought that the name Pocahontas was cute. I explained to her that she was an Indian pony and said, "I'll lead her to the creek and water her now."

Cindy started a little argument that I should bring Pocahontas water because the horse's feet were crippled just like hers. As I started leading the little mare to the creek, I said in a very casual way, "Well, walking on them might do her some good."

Cindy had coal-black hair about shoulder length and big dark eyes that made her bleached skin from the lack of sunshine look even whiter than it was. I looked back and Cindy had come across the alley and was trying to follow me and Pocahontas but she didn't have her crutches with her and it was easy to see that walking was difficult no matter what. I stopped and waited for her to catch up with us. As she rubbed the little mare's neck and ran her hands through her mane, I handed her the lead rope and said, "Miss Cindy, why don't you take Pocahontas to water."

As she took the rope in one hand, there was a pleased expression on her face that I had seldom seen before. Well, they were pretty well gaited together since neither of them could walk very fast, and Miss Cindy, without knowing it, was holding to Pocahontas's neck as they braced each other and started on to the water.

I turned and unsaddled the horse I was riding and put her in the corral and watched and waited for the two to come back up the hill. They were a long time because Pocahontas would graze and Cindy wouldn't make her move except when Pocahontas wanted to, but after a while they made it back to the barn. Cindy seemed to be walking without being so conscious of her own crippled feet.

I kept the water cut off at the corral and Cindy was taking Pocahontas to the creek two or three times a day without her folks knowing about it, so nobody was scolding her for walking too much. I noticed in a week's time that she had rubbed all the rough spots of hair on Pocahontas down to a fine gloss and that Cindy's pale little face had begun to show some color.

I decided I had better tell Dr. Chandler what I had done, so I went by his office right after dinner. He was rared back against his rolltop desk in an old high-back swivel chair sound asleep. I didn't disturb him and sat down to wait. Finally he raised up and asked how long I had been there. I told him that I had a confession to make and he said he was a doctor not a preacher, but he would listen to whatever sins I had committed.

I went into detail about my mare, Pocahontas, and his patient, Cindy. The old doctor thought the story was real good and he laughed heartily about it and commented that Cindy and Pocahontas were putting something over on her parents. He said he would find some excuse to drop by and visit and take a look at Cindy's feet and for me to come back tomorrow.

The next day about the same time I came in and roused him from his nap and he sat there, looked at me and smiled and said, "Ben, I don't know whether I want to take you in as a partner or just trade for that Indian pony, but I sure need her in my practice. Cindy's better in several ways. She's eating better, sleeping better, and her ankles and feet show a little bit of improvement and I would say that she is much lighter hearted from being in the company of one Indian pony than she had been with her family and all the help around the house. I sure hope nothing can happen that would fix that water line in your corral."

In a little while Cindy was getting too proud of Pocahontas to be sneakin' over in my pasture and she began to take her over in her yard to graze and play. Her grandfather and father both came to me to ask if it was all right for her to have the pony for her own as company and to tell me how much care they would give the pony. I told them right quick to leave Cindy and the pony alone—that she could keep her and play with her as much as she saw fit, but that the pony had been foundered and I didn't want them buying any feed to feed her to make her worse or taking too good of care of her as they had Cindy.

I decided I ought to work on Pocahontas's feet and straighten them up as much as I could, so with Cindy watchin', I sawed the dead long ends of her feet off with a saw and pared around inside of the hooves to where the frog of the hoof would get a little pressure from the ground when Pocahontas walked. Cindy watched all this and talked about it and patted Pocahontas and told her that we were doing it to help her and it would make her feet better.

Dr. Chandler told me in a few days that Cindy had asked him if he couldn't straighten her feet the way I had fixed Pocahontas's and he had given Cindy some special shoes to wear. The old family doctor hadn't missed a trick; he had had the local bootmaker fix Cindy some little sandals that would support her big toes and the insides of her feet in such a way that she would get more even weight on her instep of her foot and wouldn't walk so much on the sides and on her little toes. They were just sandals and were light and comfortable to wear in the hot weather.

Pocahontas never had a bridle on and rarely ever a lead rope. I had fixed a strong leather strap with a buckle on it that Cindy had Pocahontas wear loosely around her neck and when you saw them out for a stroll, they were always walking side by side with Cindy holding on to Pocahontas's neck. Cindy and Pocahontas became a familiar sight up and down the street from her house to the community grocery store and people would ask her why she didn't ride her pony. I don't know what her standard answer was, but they walked side by side as she held on to Pocahontas and as Pocahontas leaned some toward her.

By late fall, Dr. Chandler had changed Cindy's sandals to shoes several times and they were doing her far more good. Cindy had grown up and out and gained weight and her color was good and her dark eyes flashed as she smiled and talked about Pocahontas. Of course, the little mare had fallen in love with Cindy and nickered to her every time she went to the house and whenever she heard her voice. I had no real use for Pocahontas that would have justified taking her away from Cindy, and as winter came on, Cindy's folks built a little shed behind the garage at their house so Pocahontas could be in the warm and dry during the winter.

That fall Cindy started to public school for the first time. After school she and Pocahontas would walk together either to town or just around the neighborhood and everybody had learned to pat and brag on Pocahontas, which made Cindy beam. Cindy outgrew the physical need for Pocahontas by another summer, but she never outgrew her love for the little mare. She was constantly having a horseshoer or a veterinarian see what they could do for Pocahontas's feet and kept her until she passed away about the same time that Cindy was a teenage young lady taking dancing lessons.

BRETHREN
HORSE
TRADERS

Early one fall I had a lot of cattle in the feed lot that I intended to feed until the following spring, which would be at least five or six months. I was mixin' feed on the floor of the feed barn with a scoop and seed fork and then loadin' it onto a one-horse wagon and working my saddle mare, Beauty, to the wagon to put the feed out in the troughs. She wasn't likin' pullin' that wagon and I wasn't likin' for her to have to.

It was first Monday and I decided I'd buy a work team for this winter feeding job. There were plenty of teams around on the trade square either harnessed and hitched to wagons or standin' tied to traders' wagons waitin' for somebody to want to see 'em hooked. There was a pair of well-matched bay horses about the right size, six and seven years old, full brothers, that a well-dressed old man was drivin' around hitched to an empty wagon. He was puttin' on right smart of a spiel about how good a team they were.

There was another fellow that had about as good a pair of horses but had a little better-lookin' harness on 'em. He had been tryin' to sell his team at about the same price as the old gentleman, and there was little or no difference in the manner and appearance of these two horse owners and teams. I guess the reason that I had looked at these two teams the most was that they were already hitched to wagons and were being driven around, where most of the other traders' stock were tied to wagons and you had to pick out what you wanted and get 'em hooked up. It was early in the day and I thought as the sun got lower that the price might go down, so I didn't hurry to give either of these old gentlemen $165 for their team of horses.

I rode uptown to a chili joint and ate dinner and stopped back by at the wagonyard and was tellin' three or four fellows about needin' a team and about the two teams I had found and how little difference there seemed to be between them. Mr. Nix spoke up to say if one team suited me as well as the other, he believed he would buy the team that the best man had because more dependence could be put on his word about their pullin' quality and disposition. Then, Cat Medford said he had looked at both teams and felt like he ought to tell me that the lighter-colored pair was owned by an old retired preacher and the other team was owned by a singin' school teacher and he didn't believe he'd put any store by either of 'em's word.

Mr. Nix shamed him for such a remark and said in that case either team would probably be all right. Clint Hardin spoke up and said that if he was goin' to have to listen very much to either one of them, he'd rather listen to the singin' school teacher than the preacher and we all had a big laugh about that.

I wasn't offerin' nothing in trade and I wasn't buyin' these horses for tradin' purposes, so I was being a little more careful than I normally would have been just swappin' and sellin'. I rode back down to the trade square and looked around at some of the other horses but didn't find any matched teams that looked as good in harness as these that I had in mind. I rode around and made loose conversation till past the middle of the afternoon. That's when more people begin to tend to business and there was a chance that these two teams might both get away, so I decided I'd better make up my mind.

I offered the preacher $150 for his team and he gave me a little talkin' to about honesty; he said he hadn't put a false price on his horses and he didn't intend to take off anything. Well, that kind of a speech didn't sound good to a young horse trader, so I rode over to the wagonyard.

The singin' school teacher looked like he had a prospect and I didn't say anything until this would-be buyer walked off. I offered him $150 for his team and he hemmed and hawed and changed feet and talked about what a good team they were. He said he thought they were worth more than he had 'em priced at and he hesitated to take less. I asked him about sellin' me the harness with 'em (I didn't really need the harness), and I put in a little conversation that it looked to me like the harness was pretty small and tight for horses of this size. He said that he wanted to keep his harness because it *just* fit a pair of mules he was workin' and that it was awful tight on these good big horses.

One horse seemed to be a little uncomfortable. His britchin' was taken up real short to the tongue and you could tell by lookin' at the ground where he stood that he had moved his hind feet around a lot. Well, I had watched this music man drive this team during the day and they drove nice and were well matched and walked good with each other. After a little more light conversation I walked off, but not off so far that he couldn't come hunt me up on the other side of the trade square.

About an hour before sundown, he found me and said he hadn't had a better bid and if I would split the difference with him, he would sell me the horses. Well, I thought the daylight was in my favor and I'd just outstay him for that other $7.50 and told him I had bid all I wanted to give for 'em. He said, "Well, pay me, and I'll unharness them and you can have them."

I counted out $150 in bills, and it seemed to me that he was awfully anxious to get that money jobbed down in his pocket before he started unhookin' the team.

When you unhook a team from a wagon, you usually unhitch the traces from one horse and step behind him and reach over the tongue and unhook the traces on the other horse. But this wasn't the way he did it. He completely unhooked and unharnessed one horse and put my halter on him. I was sittin' horseback and he handed me the halter rope. I thought this was odd, but I just said to myself, "That's just another man's way of unhookin' horses." He took the bridle off the other horse and put my halter on him and handed me the halter rope with the horse still hooked to the wagon. He had a hard time pullin' the britchin' straps off and gettin' enough slack from the rein. Then he unhooked the breast yoke and slipped the harness and collar off the horse and slapped him on the rump so he would move up and I could lead them off. When he did, this last horse walked straight with his front end but his hind end kind of trailed off sideways, so much so that it was very noticeable, and directly his hind end changed sides and bumped into the other horse, then I knew for sure I was in real trouble. I thought to myself, "That old boy's probably hittin' High C for the cheatin' he's given me."

I started to the wagonyard with 'em and the right-hand horse with the loose rear end had to brace himself against the other horse to walk since he didn't have all that tight harness and wasn't strapped to the wagon tongue. As my luck would have it, I met John Barber as I started toward the wagonyard gate and he laughed in his best voice and said, "Benny, what are you goin' to do with that 'bobby'?"

I had heard of "bobbies" but I'd never seen one. A horse that has been injured in the coupling in the hindquarters and the loin and doesn't have good control of his hindquarters is referred to as a "bobby," and he is worthless unless you want to drive him in a tight harness to an empty wagon. About this time I remembered what Cat Medford had said about buyin' horses from a singin' school teacher.

Jess Manus had a pen of horses and mules in the wagonyard next to where I put my team and later in the afternoon he bought the preacher's horses. The preacher had backslid a little bit on that speech about price and had sold 'em to Jess for $140. The next morning I came down to the wagon-yard before Jess got there, I heard an awful noise and glanced over in his pen. There was the explanation for the preacher changin' his mind about the price: the best lookin' of the two horses—if there was any difference in 'em—was standin' over the water trough tryin' to suck a little water and was roarin' with an awful case of the heaves. There was a faint smell of turpentine that the old preacher had used to shut the heaves down for a few hours.

Cat Medford walked up and looked over the fence at 'em and had a good laughin' spell. He put a fresh dip of snuff in his mouth and turned like he was leavin' in a hurry, so I asked, "Cat, where you goin'?"

As he blew a little cloud of dry snuff, he said, "I'm goin' to hunt Mr. Nix and find out who's the best man in this case."

TEXAS
COW HORSES
AND THE
VERMONT
MAID

The Texas Cowboys' Reunion at Stamford, Texas, when it was first begun was a real western, enjoyable holiday. Cowboys gathered from far and near—working cowboys along with old-timers that had been good cowboys —all gathered at Stamford and had a two- or three-day rodeo. The chuck wagons from Swenson's, SMS, the Four Sixes, the Pitchfork—and I don't know who-all—would come in and feed all the visitin' cowboys. It was an unorganized kind of free-for-all rodeo held strictly for working cowboys before there were too many professionals in the business. The

only rules that these rodeos were governed by were the un-written rules of fair play that range cowboys of that day had worked by all their lives. Of course, the area boss, Scandalous John Selman, an old-time ranch foreman, had the final say if there was a tie in any of the contests.

Well, I was standin' out a way from the SMS chuck wagon—oh, just a little distance under the lacy shade of a mesquite tree by my horse—eatin' dinner. And when I say dinner, I mean it was high noon and I was eatin' barbecued beef and beans and potatoes and sourdough biscuits—the stuff that cowboys could do a day's work on—and it was sure good. Behind me was a pair of big dun chuck-wagon mules that would attract anybody's attention. I looked up, and Will Rogers was walkin' over toward me and these mules.

He looked at the mules, then he turned and started by me and 'course stopped and said "Howdy." He said, "You're ridin' a good horse."

I said, "Yessir, I've got some good horses. I've had some horses that you wound up with in years past."

He stuck out his hand and said, "I'm Will Rogers. What's your name?"

"I'm Ben Green. You bought some polo horses from some Texas shippers out in California a few years back that I trained."

He turned all smiles, and we went to talkin'. Sure enough, he'd had a Rollie Bred horse that Rollie White from Brady, Texas, had bred, called Big Enough. I'd put the schoolin' on 'im. He had liked Big Enough and remembered all about him and how good he had handled, so we were big friends in just a few minutes. I didn't waste any time in tellin' him that my ranch was covered with good young horses that were sound and clean and ready to do anything that you wanted to do on horseback—and that the market was awful bad—and what did he think about me shippin' a load of them out to California?

"Well, Ben," he said, "don't do that. The West Coast is

covered with good horses. There's a whole lot of people out there in show business that ain't eatin' too regular. Their horses suffer 'fore they do. You know them manicured cowboys that we got around these show places, the first thing they can do without when times gits hard is a horse. To begin with, they just wanted him 'cause somebody else had one. If you was to give me another horse, I don't know what I'd do with him. I'm gonna have to bob the tails on the ones I got now to make room to shut the corral gate."

We talked on about how the polo market had got bad since people had run out of spendin' money. And when I said "spendin' money," he said, "What other kind of money is they?"

We kinda laughed about that, and I told him that the government wasn't buying any remount horses and that I had spent all winter abreakin' a good bunch of horses that had slicked off in the spring—and they was shod—and I wasn't ahavin' any buyers. I had begun to hurt. He asked, "Are they as good as this horse you're aridin'?"

I said, "Yeah, I've got two more with me as good as him— and some more at the ranch."

Along about then I wasn't to impressed with Will Rogers as a national figure. I thought of him as a good cowboy that had made his way into pictures, show business, and radio— and was a good polo player and a good fellow. After all, I lived in the brush and didn't have a radio and didn't hear him very often and didn't see much about him except in a picture show or somethin'—but Will Rogers was highly regarded by all cowboys and horsemen; so after a few minutes of conversation it seemed like I had known him all my life. And the fact that he had had some horses I'd schooled made him have a good feelin' toward me, I guess.

About that time he brightened up and said, "You know, there ain't but one place that these Texas horses might sell. They're having a little flare of polo in the New England states, up around Boston and on the Eastern Seaboard. If you had the nerve to git that far from home, you might take a carload of horses up there and do pretty good with them. Outside of that, I don't know of anyplace right now where good horses of this kind are in demand—that is, by anybody that's got the money to pay for 'em."

I told Will I'd never been that far from home; I didn't know if I could stand the expense with a load of cow horses. I said I guessed I could scuffle up the money, but supposin' I didn't sell 'em and started into one of them hard New England winters. It would be a bad place to make a winter camp, wouldn't it?

He laughed and said that was something to think about. And about that time Walt Cousins, one of the men who started the Cowboys' Reunion, hollered at Will and waved him to come on. As Will left he said, "Ben, if you decide to ship up into that country and it looks like you ain't gonna git out 'fore the snow flies, git me word. I'll try to git yore horses out. I'd hate to lose a bunch of good Texas horses in one of them Yankee winters."

It was a big rodeo and he was a special guest, and about as close as I ever got to him again was when he would wave at me from somewhere—but that kind of an offer from Will Rogers was better than a contract with some men.

When I got home I wrote a few letters to the Chambers of Commerce and the sheriffs of those little towns up in Vermont, New Hampshire, and Maine. Didn't write a very good letter, I guess—didn't none of them answer me for a long time. Finally I got a letter from a place up in Vermont. The man said that they had lots of horse activity. Of course they had very fine New England horses, but if I should care to ship up there, they would be glad to have me. He had a fifty-acre meadow with a barn and some paddocks and a small cottage on it that he'd be glad to rent me while I was up there.

Well, I knew what a meadow and a barn was. That "paddock" kinda throwed me. I had to figure on it awhile, and soon I remembered they called a corral a paddock. I decided I might just as well be up there with a bunch of horses as to stay at home where everybody had horses all around so I went to makin' arrangements to ship my stock out on the train to Vermont.

And it run back through my mind, too, that Will said if I didn't do any good to get him word. That was the same as a ticket back home.

I had a half-breed Apache Indian friend named Frank. He was a good horseman, a good trainer, a little younger than me, and didn't mind hard work. He said he never had seen that country where the first Pilgrims went to taking the land away from his folks and he would kinda like to go with me. I made a trade with him, and we shipped out in a Palace stock car like you used to could rent from the American Express Company. The car was divided into stalls for your stock and feed, and it had a space for you to sleep and even do a little cookin' if you was amind to. A Palace stock car was a real nice thing, and we put twenty horses in ours.

We was nine days shippin' from Texas to Vermont. The horses hadn't drawn too much, but we went to workin' them in this Vermont mountain meadow and tryin' to get their muscles toned up and get the hair good on them. We spent five or six days brushin' and curryin' horses and bathin' in this nice little jobbed-up-close-together house called a cottage. Nobody came around or showed any curiosity about what we was doin'. It seemed we had snuck in and nobody knew we was there—for the amount of visitors we had.

I put a sign on the gate down by the road: POLO HORSES FOR SALE. That didn't seem to excite anybody, either. We had seen people in town with riding clothes on—them round-topped, hard boots with flat heels and leather-lined knees on their britches—such a bunch of fancy horse people. There was even one old man with a derby hat. I wondered how he would have ever kept that thing on in the brush with a good workin' horse. But none of these people seemed to pay us Texas cowboys any mind. Oh, you might see 'em kinda cut their eyes and look back at us when they passed. Of course, the druggist in town was pretty neighborly, and so was the man at the feed store—but we weren't having anybody to come and see our horses.

About the second Sunday morning we were there, a man drove up in a great long black automobile with big headlights stickin' out of the front fenders. He was by himself, about sixty years old, and had on riding clothes—them fancy kind that looked like they was pressed and cleaned but never used. I was cleaning out the forefoot of a horse, and I just looked up and said howdy when he stepped out of his car. He spoke to me and when I dropped the horse's foot, he took a glove off a nice, soft, pretty, smooth white hand and stuck it out and said, "I'm Charles Brent."

I said, "Howdy, Mr. Brent. I'm Ben Green. I hope you'd be interested in lookin' at some of our horses. I'll be glad to show 'em to you, and there's not anybody ahead of you." I kinda laughed when I said it.

"I'm in show business in Boston. I was talking to Will Rogers on the phone and he told me you were up in this country and for me to look you up."

I said, "Well, I'm glad to hear from Will. What else did he say?"

"He said you'd have a bunch of good horses that would be in good condition to play polo or do anything else you might want them to do. He said they would make nice light hunters for ladies, too. He also told me you could teach a horse to climb a stair, run an elevator, or write in Spanish— but he was afraid you didn't know much about how to sell one. I thought I would come up here and buy before you learn how to sell a horse."

I said, "Well, Will might be atellin' you the truth about me not knowing how to sell a horse. I've rode more of 'em than I've sold." I was takin' horses out and showin' them to him and givin' him a little talk on each one.

He finally told Apache Frank to get his saddle out of the

back of his long car—it was a Pierce-Arrow—and put it on one of these horses. He had picked out a nice blood bay horse with some white markings, sort of flashy and about fifteen hands high, one of the better horses in my load. He had a flat saddle, and there wasn't much to it. You could have rolled it up and wadded it under your arm, but it sure was fine leather and it was well kept. We got his riggin' on and held the horse steady. I thought we might be gonna have to get a block and tackle to help this big fat old man on; but he walked up by the side of this horse and just stepped up in that saddle like a kid. He took the reins in his left hand, rode the horse off in a walk, and in just a few minutes he was riding him in a figure eight, having him change leads just like he wanted him to. He was a real old-time horseman.

He rode off out in the meadow and came back, stepped off the horse, and said, "I think I'll buy this horse, but I'll be back next Sunday to try him out again." He added, "The people in the East are going to want to try your horses; they are not going to come here to buy and sell and trade as you do in the West. They may be a little hard to separate from their money."

I said, "I guess you are a typical individual, maybe. You don't want to buy one either, you want to try him out again next week." But I said it nice.

"Yes, that is right. I'm not a Yankee, however, I'm a Canadian. I moved to Boston after I was grown."

I said, "Well, Canada is farther away from Texas than Boston; so I guess that makes you worse instead of better."

He thought that was funny, and then he told me, "I don't like that sign you have on your gate. I'm in show business, and I know something about signs. Take that thing down and put a big sign up there saying, TEXAS COW HORSES, GOOD FOR EVERYTHING—see if you don't have more visitors than you are getting now."

I wasn't doing very good; so I thought it might be a good suggestion. We visited for a little while, and I told him if he

talked to Will anymore to tell him that this country was cool
and green and pretty, that the people were cool, too, and
that the horse business was damn poor.

Next morning I went down to the drugstore and told my
druggist friend I wanted to find a sign painter. He sent me
to an old man in a little shop on the side street. Of course
the old man spoke that New England lingo—not much
humor and not too much conversation—but he found out
what kind of sign I wanted. He said he would have to paint
a board white about three times, then he would paint the
letters on it, and it would be ready on Wednesday. He didn't
hesitate to tell me it would cost ten dollars.

I told him I thought I could stand that, so just go ahead
and get it fixed so it would attract attention and people would
come to see my horses. Meantime, one or two people came to
look at horses—and they were great lookers. They would
walk around these horses, look in their mouths, pick up their
feet, and feel them all over. They seemed to think they were
going to get cheated—and I don't believe it's possible to
cheat one of them Yankees. I had a whole lot of experience
there, and they sure do turn loose of their money slow.

I went back to the old man's on Wednesday and, sure
enough, the sign was ready. I gave him his ten dollars. I didn't
have any means of transportation except horseback, so I
carried this sign under my arm out to where we nailed it up
pretty high over the gate. It said: TEXAS COW HORSES, BROKE
GENTLE TO DO ANYTHING YOU WANT TO DO HORSEBACK. The
old man had drawn a few little cartoons around on it of
Texas cowboys—or what he thought they looked like. I didn't
like them much, but I figured nobody else would know what
Texas cowboys looked like and it wouldn't make any difference. I was hoping the people could read, anyway, and would
know what the sign said.

Just a little after noon—me and Frank had beat up a
bachelors' dinner—up drove a station wagon plumb full of
girls. The one adrivin' stepped out on the ground—she had

on these fancy riding clothes—and introduced herself. She said she had a summer camp and riding academy up on the other end of the meadow, about two or three miles from us. The other girls were her students. They had seen the sign POLO HORSES, but that hadn't interested them too much. It seemed that nearly everybody had polo horses, but Texas cow horses were something they weren't used to seeing.

This was a real good-looking blue-eyed gal, not very big, with soft, dark brown hair and the blackest eyebrows and eyelashes you ever saw. To a cowboy from way out West —even though she was wearing the wrong kind of riding britches—she looked good. All the rest of these gals piled out of the station wagon, and they were a lively set of good-looking kids. They went to walking up and down the barn, talking, and asking about our horses. Apache Frank made a big hit with all of them right fast. He was a natural-born lady-killer without trying. I was pretty much on the timid side, and I was tending to business. I was hoping I had a buyer in that bunch of girls.

This young lady that seemed to be the ramrod of the whole show, she was quite a horsewoman—you could tell right off. She took a fancy to a horse, and I led him out of the stall and showed him to her. The girls went to running their hands around over that horse and talking about how he hadn't been "groomed." I didn't know for sure how much more rubbin' that meant, but we thought we were taking pretty good care of them. The good-looking gal in charge kinda reprimanded these girls a little bit—but you could tell she had taught them just exactly what they were tellin' us, that our horses hadn't been "groomed." I didn't know if a Texas horse would stand for that much polish or not.

We took some more horses out of the stalls, and we had some flat saddles that they grabbed and went to puttin' on. They saddled up properly and then went to mountin' that bunch of horses like so many flies. There weren't any help-less females in that bunch. The teacher just watched and let them play around. Once in a while she would call out and correct one of them about the way she was holding the reins, or wasn't sitting down in the saddle, or wasn't holding her toes out, or something else that didn't make any difference, it didn't seem to me.

Late that afternoon, this gal teacher said, she would be holding regular classes. They would just be delighted to have us come up and look at their horses and perhaps I could offer some suggestions in "equitation." Well, that was something I hadn't heard about, so I told her I didn't expect I would know anything she hadn't taught them already, but that we would come see their horses—what time would she suggest?

She said, "We have two classes this afternoon, from four o'clock until dinner. We'd be glad to have you stay for dinner."

This gettin' dinner at dark was another little riffle that West Texas cowboys wasn't used to. I just wondered—up in that high mountain meadow country, in that tall green grass and cool breezes—maybe they did a lot of things different from us.

Of course Apache Frank had his ear up, and he told the rest of the gals he would sure be there. With this, they all went to loading up in that station wagon and waving and hollering "We'll be looking for you" and all that stuff. It seemed to us this Yankee country might be gonna take on a little better complexion.

Of course Frank asked me right off, "That grooming business, what did they mean?" So after a while we got out two of the best horses we had and we groomed them some more before we rigged them out with Texas stock saddles. We weren't gonna ride them flat saddles up there.

We rode up the road about two and a half or three miles and, sure enough, here was this palatial kind of summer camp—nice bunk house, a big kitchen, a dining room, and something Frank called a parlor (we found out later they called it a rumpus-room). And they had some horses we weren't quite used to. They were Eastern-bred horses and weren't shaped like ours and didn't look exactly like ours— and they were sure enough groomed; there wasn't a hair out of place. Their saddles were set just right, and you could tell they had been putting that saddle soap on the bridle reins and the head stalls that were made out of English leather—stuff we weren't used to. They talked about "tack" this and "tack" that. It took Frank and me a little while to catch on, but the Indian was sharper than I was. He figured out that all that "tack" stuff meant riggin' something. We had to listen to that New England English awhile before we could carry on a real good conversation—and I wouldn't say it was plumb good then, but at least we got it around to where they could understand us a little better.

They rode these horses around in figure eights, circled them, and changed leads. This gal that I was by that time kinda snortin' at, was agivin' out the orders about pull-in-your-left-rein, stick-out-your-right-toe, and one thing and another. Sounded kinda silly to me, but she was sure enough gettin' those gals to sit on those horses. This was all a new world to me in the horse business, and I was gettin' an eyeful of it.

The second class was jumpers. I tell you these girls could sure ride a jumper. They had those little old flat saddles and double reins. Those old ponies would clear those poles and hit the ground on the other side and the gals, it looked like, just rode the breeze. I could tell right off that maybe they couldn't ride a cow horse, but the kind they knew about they were doing a real good job on. Of course, I didn't hesitate to tell this to this good-looking gal—the boss of the bunch. I was beginning to give her some sweet talk, and she wasn't fightin' me too much when I was braggin' on her horses and braggin' on her students.

Well, after a while we went in to this dinner. The cook was an old woman with her hair drawed up tight in a knot on the back of her head, but she was nice and she said she was glad to have company. They had a big dinner. Of course they had it at suppertime, and it was a little hard for me not to say supper. Anyway, we got through that all right, and kinda late we said our good-byes and got on our horses and went back to camp. On the way home we walked along kinda slow, and I went to telling Frank that I believed this summer deal might be all right if we could just sell some horses, too.

By Sunday that sign was astoppin' everybody. They were coming to see Texas cow horses. They were feeling of them and talking about them; it was a little hard for me to understand that Yankee lingo, but I was catching on a little more all the time. They said some things about horses that I didn't quite savvy, but they were sure strong on "trying" these horses. They would try them and try them and come back the next day and try them some more—and bring two or three more people with them to offer opinions about each horse. On Saturday of the week that I had put the sign up on Wednesday, I sold my first horse—for cash—and got $300 for him.

Well, he was worth about $150 in Texas; I guess I had $50 more in him for expenses, so I was about to make a $100; and that would be the first money we'd seen since we got there.

I was cleaning off horses Sunday morning when up drove Mr. Brent. He got out of this long black Pierce-Arrow and said, "I see you have changed your sign."

I said, "Yeah, and it's making a lot of difference in my business. I'm not sellin' any horses, but I'm havin' lots of lookers."

"That 'Texas Cow Horses' will make any of these boys up here come to look. They don't know but what a Texas cow horse is a Spanish pony, and I am sure they have been surprised to learn that you have some nice horses with breeding and size."

I said, "Oh, we've had lots of compliments on our horses and lots of visitors and lots of tryin'—but I've sold one horse."

"I think it will get better. These New Englanders are pretty clannish. You would not have had more lookers if the first one had not found something."

I said, "Shore 'nuff?"

"Yes. You are in a strange land—to you. But these people will probably all buy horses before they wear you out looking at them."

I said, "I sure hope so." Then I told him about the girls at the camp coming down and looking and that we had been going up there—and that some of our horses were up at the camp now where the girls were going to try to teach them to be hunters or jumpers.

That brightened him up considerably; and when he realized that I might have some business, he looked at this good bay horse that he had ridden the Sunday before and said, "I think I'll ride this horse again today."

I said, "Fine," and we got his rigging out of the car and saddled up the horse for him. He rode a little while and came back and got down and went to cleaning the horse off himself. He took the saddle off and went to rubbing this horse down and sponging off his legs. (We had got a sponge. We had begun to catch on to this grooming business.) I told him Frank would do that.

"No," he said. "I always groom my own horse."

"Well, that's fine, but I didn't know this was your own horse."

"Yes," he said, "he will be. However, we may have to discuss money. Your figure may be too high."

"No, I don't think so. He's the best horse we've got and I'm gonna sell him dirt cheap. I just want $500 for him."

He threw his sponge over in a bucket of water and went to kinda shaking his hands out in the air. Then he reached in his pocket and got a spotless white handkerchief out and wiped his hands off. He said, "I detest sponging another man's horse on Sunday."

"You sure did swap that horse off quick, didn't you, since

I told you $500? It's just like I said, Canada's farther away from Texas than this Yankee country is, and I guess they get tougher the farther north you go."

He didn't dare laugh—he hadn't near decided not to buy this horse. He just smiled a little and said he felt like he could afford $350 for the horse.

I told him I was sure glad he was in good circumstances, but that I couldn't take $350. He was going to have to afford $400.

He stomped around awhile. Finally he said, "If you weren't a friend of Will Rogers, I wouldn't pay it."

I said, "If that was my excuse, you ought to pay me $1,000 and I could send Will part of it."

He just laughed and wrote me out a check for $400 and said that he would send his man up with a truck sometime during the week and pick up the horse. I sure thanked him— and by that time there were a few more people around the barn looking at horses. They all had on those fancy Sunday riding clothes, those pantaloon britches, and hard-topped, flat-heeled boots. Some of them had been there before, and they were making themselves quite at home.

One horse there had been tried by the same man five times. We had ridden this horse the day before, and the girls had jumped him the day before that. So when this man said he was going to try the horse again, I said, "No, I don't believe you are unless you are gonna buy him. You've tried that horse enough, and he has been ridden pretty hard this week. I'd prefer that you didn't try him unless you are gonna pay for him."

Well, this kinda ruffled him a little bit. He kinda growled and said this was a very impolite way to treat a guest. I said that I didn't know horse traders were ever guests, but in my country you don't ever try a horse that many times, so I just believed we would turn the horse back in the barn.

This made him mad, but he had a friend with him, so he said, "Do you still want $400?"

I said, "Yes sir."

"I wouldn't give you but $300."

I said, "That would be enough. Just give it." He didn't know it, but I only had $50 and expenses in that horse that lacked a whole lot being my best horse. I was afraid if this man kept on tryin' him, he might find out that the horse wasn't so good; so we sold him right quick.

Mr. Brent was listening to all this. "Ben," he said, "you are being too abrupt with these people. Talk like that might be all right in Texas, but it won't go over here."

I said, "To hell it won't. Here's the man's check."

Mr. Brent laughed and got in his car and said he would see me again.

The next week passed off fast. We were having the time of our lives up at the girls' camp teachin' riding lessons or ataking riding lessons or rompin' and stompin' and playin' in the meadows of the green mountain country of Vermont. One night we fixed them a big Texas barbeque down at our barn. Even the old woman cook came. They just had more fun, and everybody laughed and hollered and squealed and took on.

Then on Sunday the parents of all these young gals came out to watch their horse show—the likes of which I had never seen before. They introduced Frank and me as Texas cowboys, and we showed the people how a reining horse reined. We roped and cut and ran back and forth—of course they didn't have any cattle there to demonstrate on, but we roped a few fenceposts. Then I ran by Frank and he roped my horse, and he ran by me ahorseback and I roped his. They thought that was marvelous, I guess. They just never heard of such a thing.

While I was playing with my rope dropped loose, one of my horses got out of the barn and ran into the arena. As he ran past me, I just caught him by the forefeet with my loop. The whole crowd just ohed and ahed. Of course that old pony had been caught by the forefeet lots of times, and he froze in his tracks. He never made another move until I walked up to him, slipped the other end of the rope around his neck, and took the loop off his feet. You never heard anything like that cheering when I led him out of the arena. You would have thought these people were at the biggest rodeo ever held at Pecos, Texas.

Before the parents went home that day, they just about bought the rest of our horses. We had more business than you could think about. These people weren't too hard to separate from their money because their girls had been riding and using our horses and trying them out. Each girl knew which horse she wanted, and some of the mothers and fathers were buying horses for themselves.

By this time I was getting pretty far along with this blue-eyed Vermont maid, this cute filly that was the teacher. I didn't stop to notice whether she was older or younger than I was, and Apache Frank was busy being a ladies' man and entertaining all the young ones. But this blue-eyed, black-lashed Vermont maid had gotten me over a lot of that bashfulness that cowboys are afflicted with.

People don't generally know it, but cowboys who are raised out in the range country and stay with a chuck wagon and grow up kinda wild—such cowboys don't know much about gals. They just know that some of them are pretty and others sound nice and most of them smell good. There are lots of things young cowboys don't know about gals, and this was pretty much my condition that summer I set out for Yankee country with my load of cow horses.

But she had begun to get me over my timidness, and I had learned a lot about the fair sex from this Vermont maid. She would get her classes over in the mornings, and then she would take the station wagon and come down by our barns. I would have my horses worked out and exercised; I'd leave Frank agroomin' his horses; and she and I would drive down to town and sip soda and laugh and tell jokes and have fun. I sure thought I was doing awful good with her. I had traded her a horse, too. She had a Morgan stallion that was a little too much for these girls. He was a little rank and hard-mouthed, and they were too light-armed to be able to handle him; so she traded him to me for a nice dun gelding.

Well, this dun gelding was quite a horse. He was only fourteen-two hands high, and we called him Quickie. The girls thought that was a cute name for a horse, and they had all been aridin' Quickie. But they got to using him in pole-bending contests, and he was pretty trigger-happy on that bridle rein. This pole-bending contest was something new for a cowboy. They never did bend a pole. That wasn't the idea. It ought to have been called a horse-bending con-test, because they would line these poles up and run a horse through them, reining him and bending him between the poles; and when they got to the end of the poles, they would turn the horse and run him back through this line of poles. Well, this dun horse was just so fast on the turns—that's why we called him Quickie—that anytime you touched him you'd better be settin' good and tight 'cause he was fixin' to do something.

Well, Quickie had spilled just about every gal up there that was trying to ride him on those flat saddles, and they were getting a little unhappy with him. But, still, my teach-filly had traded for him—and she got to asking me why he couldn't be slowed down. I told her that cowboys spent a lifetime trying to put a rein on a horse, teaching him to be quick, and there wasn't any point in trying to get him over it. This made sense to her, but she was not happy about that horse trade.

Well, I wasn't going to trade her back this Morgan stal-lion. The Morgan horse breed originated in Vermont from a little stud named Justin Morgan. A Vermonter by the name of Richard (Dick) Selman came to Texas in an early day and brought with him many pure Vermont Morgan horses. I worked on the Selman Ranch near Brady, Texas, as a boy—breaking weanling colts to lead at a time when there were more than four hundred Morgan horses on the Selman Ranch. Now I had a Morgan stud that was the start of a herd of Morgans for me—and I didn't want to trade this stud for anything.

One morning we had gone downtown to sip a little soda and be sociable, and she brought Quickie up again. She wished I would trade back for him. I had to tell her then how proud I was of this Morgan stud and that I hoped to trade for two or three Morgan mares to take back to Texas with me and start a little band of Morgan horses. This interested her. She smiled and said, "Then it is all right. We'll do something else with Quickie." And she got real nice and polite and just made me feel a little ashamed of myself for holding her to the horse trade.

But she really wasn't cheated. Her girls couldn't ride old Quickie, that's all. There was a lot of cowboys couldn't ride him, either. Quickie could turn through himself and not get out of shape—which is quite an accomplishment for a good cow horse.

Apache Frank and I were so busy having fun that we hadn't paid too much attention to what the business situation was. We had four of the horses left that we had brought with us and this Morgan stud, which meant we were nearly out of the horse business. To stay in Vermont living in style just to show four horses—that didn't make much sense. I told Frank that we were liable to be getting ready to ship out of that country. The first thing he did was to tell all these gals how they were going to miss him—he was an over-all ladies' man, I tell you. They, of course, broke the news to that blue-eyed, black-lashed Vermont maid of mine. They didn't want us to go back to Texas. Oh, they just took on and made us feel so good. They were even talking about how they would like to come to visit us some summer.

We were all for that. We just let on like we had room for all of them. But in one of those little batchin' shacks out on the ranch where we stayed, you couldn't have got their saddles and clothes in it if they had all come to visit—but that didn't worry us too much.

I had one exceptionally good horse left—a blue roan horse, fifteen hands high, weighing eleven hundred, and six years old. He was one of the most useful horses I ever owned, and I thought that since I had sold several horses real high I could afford to keep the roan and ship him back to Texas. Well, this Vermont maid took quite a shine to this horse. I didn't let Frank ride him. I kinda kept him to myself. I thought if I didn't get him sold, I didn't want any fresh teachin' put on him that wouldn't suit me.

My Vermont maid went to telling me that if we were going to ship to Texas that she sure would like to buy or trade for that blue roan. I told her he would be awful high, even to her, and she could buy him cheaper than anybody. Of course that was good conversation.

She said, "How would you trade him for some Morgan mares?"

"Well, that would be about the only thing that would get this horse. I don't think I'd swap him for United States money. I've already got a bunch of this Yankee money—more than I ever thought I'd get when I shipped up here—and I'd rather have some Yankee horses instead of more Yankee money.

She thought this was kinda funny, and so did the three or four girls who were listening. This was all happening one night at the supper—excuse me—dinner table. She said that she had two or three Morgan mares in a pasture on the back side of her place, up on the mountain, and that she would bring them in so I could see them. She just felt that I would like them.

I told her it would take about a pastureful to get this blue roan, because he was so good and I thought so much of him. The girls thought that was real funny. All these gals were always laughing at the way Frank and I expressed ourselves. They thought we talked real funny. We didn't. They were the ones that talked funny.

Of course these gals teased us a whole lot about how much horsemanship they had taught us Texas cowboys. We were always hurrahing them about how they wouldn't have learned anything at that camp if we hadn't come up there that summer. All that kind of stuff went on all the time. And once in a while I would tease them about not being able to ride old Quickie. I'd tell this Vermont maid that it was too bad she didn't know how to trade horses as well as she knew how to teach young ladies to ride. This went on all the time—it got to where didn't anybody pay too much attention to it. Just every now and then something would come up about horses that they had never heard of before, and either Frank or I would say, "Well, you just put that down as something else you learned from Texas cowboys."

About the middle of the week I let the news out that we would try to ship out Monday. I had already been down and told the railroad agent that we would want an immigrant car (that's what you call a car that carries livestock, equipment, furniture, and so forth—instead of just straight livestock). He had to order one from somewhere; they didn't ship any livestock up there by carloads. A carload of livestock going in or out of there was so unusual that you had to order a car several days ahead of time.

So I had told the gals that I thought we ought to stay over one more Sunday. They were going to have another of those Sunday horse shows. I knew it would be fun, and I wasn't worried about these last four horses we had. I knew I could sell them if I had or wanted to, and I was still kinda of the opinion that I would take this blue roan back to Texas with me.

We rode up late one afternoon to watch the gals in their late afternoon class. We were figuring on getting an invitation to stay for supp—I mean—dinner and get some more of that female cooking and conversation. That all goes together, you know. This Vermont maid said she had her Morgan mares in the barn and if we would just wait out there by the riding ring, she would bring them out. I thought that would be all right, and directly she came out on a nice, brown, typical Morgan mare—good feet and legs, a beautiful head, and a nice, short back. She rode the mare and showed her, and this mare traveled nice. Of course, she was just out of the pasture and wasn't in real good shape, but they had put the groom on her. She had every hair in place and was slick and bright and pretty. She had her fetlock trimmed and her mane and tail combed out, but other than that, she was a little out of shape, just like a grass mare would be. But she was a real nice young mare and I liked her and liked the way she traveled, and thought, "Now that will be one to take home with that stud."

As the Vermont maid started to ride the mare to the barn, she told us, "The show is not over. Wait and I'll bring out another one."

This second mare she brought out was a much better individual—a dark, dark seal brown with black feet and legs and not a white hair on her. She just traveled on and was the best mannered thing. Oh, she was nice to look at with this gal aridin' her. They cantered and figured-eight, and it sure made a pretty picture. I just thought, "That's the kind of mares I need to start a band of Morgans with. If I can just trade for them without that gal finding out how bad I want them." So I said out loud, "She's a nice mare. How old is she?"

"She's a little older than the other one."

Well, we weren't too paper-minded in those days. We hadn't learned a lot about registered horses—or I hadn't. She told me the young mare had papers, and this one didn't, but she was a true-blooded Morgan mare. That you could see at a glance. This was such a nice mare, and this favorite girl friend of mine was showing her—so I just didn't think it would be polite to walk up and pop the mare's mouth open to see how old she was. Anyway, she was a bright-headed mare that carried herself beautifully, and she couldn't be too old; so I didn't let it bother me.

She put the mare back in the barn and came out and said, "How did you like my mares?"

I said, "Well, they are sure nice. If you had about half a dozen more like that, I'd trade the blue roan horse for them."

The girls were all listening—seemed like they knew this horse trade was up—and they hooted me pretty bad when I said that. The Vermont maid rolled those big blue eyes at me and said, "You'll be lucky if you get either one of them for the horse."

Of course I knew that wasn't so, and I had a big haw-haw about that. We went in to eat, and as the evening wore on the girls were telling me how lucky I would be to get one of these mares. Everybody was trying to have a horse trade, and they were trying to trade me out of that blue roan horse for just one mare. I told them that just wouldn't do at all. They worked on it so long and so hard that I finally said I would trade for both of them. They thought this was funny—that I would say my horse was worth both mares. Of course this was all light conversation, and it looked like I wasn't getting very close to a horse trade.

Frank and I ate most of their grub; it was getting late, so we told the gals good night. This Vermont maid walked out to the hitching rack with me. Frank was about half polite. He knew when to leave so he got on his horse and rode off. She and I stood there and talked in the moonlight. She told me she would hate to see me go back to Texas and all that stuff. Sure did sound good and I ate it up. And she told me that if I really was serious about wanting to trade for those mares that I could study about it. She would give both of them for the roan. I think that was what she walked out to the hitching rack to tell me instead of all the rest of that stuff that went on.

Next morning, the whole class came down to our barn—
eighteen head of gals and horses. They just covered the
place like they always did, and we all saddled up and went
into town. The Vermont maid rode the blue roan. It created
a little excitement around town when all of us kids rode in
there horseback, and I told the gals I would take them out
on the town and buy them lunch. It was a little town and it
wasn't going to cost much. It was kinda early, and they called
the old gal back at headquarters and told her not to fix them
any lunch. You know that tickled her.

They had one of those nice old New England hotels in
town; so we went over there to eat. They served one of those
boiled dinners. It was good grub, of course a little different
from what I was used to. Anyhow, we had a big lunch and
had a big time; and after we mounted up and rode out of
town, I told my Vermont maid that I didn't think we'd come
up that afternoon. We needed to kinda clean that barn up
and kinda straighten up a little bit.

She said she would be glad to have us come up tomorrow;
so the next day we rode up there. She brought the Morgan
mares out and showed them again. They'd had a little time to
work on these mares, and the gals had sure been working on
them. The mares were getting in show shape, and the nicest
mare was traveling a lot better. They had put shoes on her;
she didn't really need them because she had good hard feet,
so they were getting her ready for something. She was sure
showing off good, and I was liking both these mares. They
actually weren't worth as much as my blue roan horse. In
fact, I thought they were worth about $200 apiece, and I
thought he was worth about $600. I hadn't decided to trade
him for these two mares yet, but I didn't know where else
to look for mares. I didn't have any way to get around much.
Anyway, I thought maybe I'd better keep that Yankee money
I'd got together and swap for mares instead of spending
money.

After all, there hadn't been anybody around that wanted

to give as much money for a horse as I wanted for this blue roan. And I just thought, With two Morgan mares and a Morgan stud, I could go home and raise a whole herd of horses. I would forget if there was any difference in value between my blue roan and these mares.

We were going to ship out on Monday morning, so Sunday afternoon we went up to the girls' horse show and stayed for supper. They showed me the Morgan mares again. Every time I looked at them, they looked better than the time before. And this older mare had the brightest head, the prettiest eyes, and carried her ears the nicest of anything I nearly ever saw.

In the meantime, I sold the other three horses. Frank was still riding one of them, but the man was going to send for him the next day. The blue roan was the only horse I actually owned except for the stud; so I just traded with the Vermont maid for these two dark brown Morgan mares. We let them out of the barn after supper—excuse me, dinner—and I left the blue roan and saddled the nicest mare with my Texas saddle. She sure did ride good. I'd never had a horse feel better under me on the road. She traveled good and reached good and had a smooth way of carrying you—and still felt stout under you. I still hadn't looked in her mouth to see how old she was.

We led the four-year-old mare and went back down to our camp. Of course it was dark, and we didn't have lights in our barn down there. We just turned the mares in the barn that night and went to bed. We lay there and talked about the gals and all the fun we'd had and how good we'd done on our horses—and that old Will sure did me a favor when he told me there might be a place up in New England where I could sell some horses. We had romped and played in the high meadows of the mountain country where the grass was green, the weather cool, and the female company delightful. It was a lot different from the searing summers a Texas cowboy usually spends handling wild cattle, bad horses, and eating camp grub thrown together by a mad, old, wore-out cowboy that had to turn cook because he couldn't ride anymore.

Our car was at the railroad station and we were ready to load out the next morning. Of course there were no shipping pens or anything like that in a little New England town. We were going to lead our horses up on the dock to load them— our Morgan mares and our stud—before the train pulled out about nine o'clock that morning. The fellow that had rented us the meadow and the barn was going to take his little pickup truck and haul our saddles and feed and other plunder that we had to load to the boxcar.

It was early morning, but we couldn't help but look back up the road to see if some of the gals were coming to see us off. We'd said our good-byes the night before, but we were hoping some of them would show up. I had my money in my pocket, and we were riding down to the depot. I was on the good mare, and Frank was riding the stud and leading the four-year-old. I was kinda adding up how good we'd done and how much fun we'd had—and there I was, going back to Texas with the purest of Morgan blood from the country Morgans started from. This all added up pretty nice, and we weren't saying anything much—just riding along.

I just noticed that this mare I was on never had let her ears down a time. Every time you looked at them, they were standing straight out looking down the road. That was a little odd. A mare ought to flop her ears back and forth a little once in a while. But that didn't bother me a whole lot. We rode up on the shipping dock, got our horses inside the boxcar, and started to build a stall in one end of the boxcar for the stallion so he wouldn't cause too much trouble. We hammered and fixed and put him back in this stall. We had a place to tie the two mares in the other end of the boxcar. It wasn't like that Palace stock car we came up in, but it had a big tank for some water for our hourses and a place to keep our feed and everything like that. We were getting pretty well fixed up. The old man had unloaded his truck, and we had paid him all we owed him. I guess he was glad to get rid of us. He'd had an awful lot of excitement around that outfit that summer.

I don't know how come me to do it—but for some reason or another I rubbed my hand up over that mare's ears. I wondered why they were standing up so straight. It hit a little hard something way down at the bottom of the ear, bedded down under the hair where you couldn't see it. I ran my hand down the ear again, and I hit it again. Then I turned and reached over and ran my hand over that other ear. It was the same way. This old mare let her head down like her ears might be hurting her. When she did, I got to looking real close. There were several strands of real fine, hard brown silk thread—just the color of that mare's head —wrapped real hard and tied real tight around the bottom of her ears to keep her ears sticking up straight. The thread was pulled so tight that the cartilage was wrinkled a little bit in the ears and set them forward—and they just set there. She couldn't have let them back if she had wanted to. I said, "Frank, lookee here."

He ran his hand over her ears and said, "What is it? I don't see nothin'."

I said, "I didn't either, but you can feel it."

He felt it, and he said, "Well, I'll be damned!"

I got my pocketknife out and I worked real careful. This mare's ears had gotten pretty sore, and they were touchy. I cut that silk thread, unwound it off of that ear, unwound it off the other ear—and you never saw the likes of thread! It took a whole lot of it. And those gals had worked that thread in there to where it didn't even show. They had that hair so bright and slick, and it lay over that thread that was so tight—but when I turned it loose, both ears just flopped every which way. That old mare had the laziest ears you ever saw —and it sure did change her expression—and mine.

While we were working around these ears, I noticed my

hands turning a dark shade of brown. I knew they had that old mare cleaned off; but the palm of my hand was a little sweaty, and I just rubbed it right hard over her head. All kinds of color came off on my hand.

That old mare was mossy-headed. You never saw as much white hair show on a mare's head, and the more I rubbed, the whiter it got. It got white down around her eyes: she was so old that she was grey-headed before those gals painted her head.

I opened her mouth. Her teeth were as long as a pencil— well, maybe not, but they sure were long.

Old Frank just fell down in that car and just lay there where we'd broken open a bale of hay and just laughed till he hurt. I was kinda sick about the deal—yet it was funny to me, too. I wasn't quite in the humor to laugh, so I finally kicked him in the ribs with my boot toe and told him to get up there and put up the bars on that boxcar door. I had heard the train whistle, and I was kinda glad it was coming. I wanted to get out of that country before I found something else wrong with my mare.

About the time the train hooked on to our car, a station wagon drove up. It was loaded with those gals, and they were awavin' and ahollerin'. I squalled at this blue-eyed, black-lashed Vermont maid and said, "What did you color that mare's head for?"

"Why, honey," she answered, "you thought that color was so beautiful on my eyelashes and eyebrows! I didn't think you would mind it on that nice mare's head."

Frank and all the gals just died laughing. But as the train pulled out I squalled at them right loud again, "Anyway, it took eighteen New England maids to cheat one Texas Cowboy."

MULE
SCHOOLIN'

I had been to Granbury and spent most of the day doin' more loafin' than business, and was on my way back to the ranch. I was ridin' a good horse named Dan and it was still the heat of the day, so I was lettin' him take his time when one of those little quick summer thunder showers built up and got me and him wet in the matter of a few minutes and then passed on and the sun came out. Well, ridin' along in the heat of the summer and gettin' a quick shower never bothered a cowboy; you wouldn't even think about changin' clothes because when the sun came out, they'd dry on you in a little bit.

I rode up to Davidson's store at Thorp Springs to break the ride home and stopped for a little local conversation and refreshment. Davidson's store was a small country mercantile sort of place with groceries and dry goods and a small amount of shelf hardware. As I ate my bar of candy and drank my Coke, Mr. Davidson set in to sell me a dry change of clothes. And I told him that would be kind of foolish, that the ones I had on would be dry in a few mintues.

I put up considerable argument that I wasn't interested in buyin' clothes every time I got wet and he pulled out a good pair of black-and-white-stripped duckin' britches and a blue duckin' shirt that would come near enough to fittin' me and told me that I could put on a change of clothes for a dollar bill. Well, that sounded like a bargain and I went in the back of the store to change clothes.

Some of the grown men of the community were sittin' up in the east door discussin' the problems of farmin', which didn't sound too entertainin' to a cowboy that wasn't interested in turnin' the grass bottom side up, so I didn't pay a lot of attention until I heard the Professor. A university professor that wasn't nearly old enough to quit teachin' had moved into the community and had said that he retired from teachin' in order to live on the land and enjoy farmin'. He was full of brilliant ideas and well impressed with his vast knowledge of general subjects and his particular knowledge

of farmin' and was generous in explainin' his views. He
always brought up the fact that education took time and
money and it was a pity there weren't more well informed
men engaged in farmin'. Well, you could tell by his conversation that he was more than willin' to share his vast knowledge with us ignorant people that had been makin' a livin'
off the land while somebody had been payin' him to learn
their children readin' and writin'.

While I was changing clothes, he began to expound on
the matter of fertilizer. He had just put out some fertilizer
and was glad to see this little shower melt and send it into
the ground. I asked Old Man Davidson what kind of manure
would melt. And he said, "Now, Ben, you ought to be smarter
than that. The Professor is referrin' to 'commercial' fertilizer
that is ground up from mineral rocks and then spread on the
ground."

I said, "Well, that might be a daintier way to enrich the
soil, but I doubt if it's ever gonna take the place of good
fresh stall horse manure."

I didn't break into the conversation that the older men
were carryin' on. I just made my respectful howdies and
went on about my business. I tied my had-been-wet clothes
on my saddle and they were nearly dry by now and as I
rode off toward the ranch, I wondered why I had let old
Davidson talk me out of that dollar.

The next time I ran on to Professor Know-It-All was at a
Sunday afternoon singin' at the country church. A bunch of
men were sittin' out under the big oak trees where they
could hear the singin' and still get in some visitin' and have
the privilege of smokin' their pipes after the big dinner that
had been served on the grounds. Professor Know-It-All took
advantage of a pretty fair gatherin' under them trees to explain how he had irrigated his garden by usin' the law of
gravity to flow the water from the windmill zigzag and cross-
ways down the hill and what a great advantage it was to
have enough education to be able to take proper advantage

of the angles that it took to flow that water with so little
fall to the ground because he had such a complete knowledge of the law of gravity. Well, I had heard something
about this gravity business and when he looked up at me
with his all-knowing smile, looking as though he expected
some sort of favorable comment, I said I wished they would
modify them damn laws of gravity so when an old bronc
threw me, I wouldn't fall so fast and so hard.

The neighbors all laughed and Professor Know-It-All said,
"Ben, you will have a greater appreciation of knowledge as
you grow older and try to learn the important things of life."

I decided the singin' in the church house would sound
better at closer range and there might be some of them
young fillies sittin' close enough to the back where I could
move into a better class of company and smell a little
perfume instead of that smoke comin' from them pipes, so
I left that bunch of brain-bustin' and went inside.

I was out of circulation for a week or more workin' cattle
before I got back to town. I went to the meat market where
they had tables in the back and you could eat all the barbecue and bread and onions that you wanted for a quarter.
I sat down on one of them long benches at the table after I
had filled my plate, and who walked in but Professor Know-
It-All. He got his meat and bread but said he would "de-
cline" the onions. Then he walked over and made me move
up the bench and he sat down on the end by me.

We carried on a little light conversation while the Professor minced around with his meat and I had my mouth full.
Directly somebody got up off the far end of one of them
benches and the man on the other end like to have fell on the
floor. After the laughin' and hurrahin' was over and the people got through chokin' on their meat, the Professor set in to
explain the law of physics and the balance of weight on that
bench, and he stressed the importance of education and the
knowledge of these complicated doings that could be simple.
Of course, he touched on the fact that education was ex-

pensive and he couldn't expect everybody to understand what he was talkin' about. When I finished my barbecue and started to leave, I told him I thought physics was a dose of medicine and he sure had enlightened me.

The next time I stopped at the store, Mr. Davidson told me that Professor Know-It-All was havin' trouble with his mules. One day when I was ridin' up the road, I met him drivin' his mules to a wagon. We stopped in the middle of the road and he told me he was havin' an awful time workin' that team of mules and felt that Mr. Bennett had taken undue advantage of him and had sold him an unbroke pair of mules. Well, I glanced at the mules and I had seen them many times before. The Professor had adorned them with a new set of leather harnesses and you could tell by the looks of the mules that he was takin' extra-good care of them.

I consoled him a little by tellin' him that I felt he and the mules would finally get used to each other and they ought to work out all right because if Old Man Bennett could work 'em, a man of his vast knowledge and education shouldn't have any trouble with 'em. This made him feel good and you could see him strut a little even though he was sittin' in the spring seat.

One day I passed the farm that Professor Know-It-All had bought and saw him drivin' his team of mules to a cultivator. The rows ran out to the road fence and turned, so I just thought I would wait for a little of that smartenin' up in the shade of a tree since he wasn't more than a hundred yards away. As I watched him comin' down the row, I could see that this nice pair of sorrel mare mules had sweated until they were breaking out in a lather and they were nervous and looked like they were tryin' to cross their heads across the tongue and were both walkin' on the middle bed.

Professor Know-It-All pulled them up at the end of the row and walked over to the shade of the tree. He was wearin' new work clothes, which most farmers saved and wore to town a few times before they went to the field in them. He set in to tell me in very properly phrased English how disgusted he was with the way his team of mules were acting that day as he tried to cultivate his corn crop. He said that they had tromped the young corn down on the middle row and in their twisting around caused him to cut down some corn with the cultivator plows. He added that he believed he was going to be forced to sell them and probably get a team of horses since he knew they were more intelligent than mules. There was just too wide a spread between what he knew and what mules knew for him to be able to work them satisfactorily.

I knew what he had given for these mules and it had dawned on me what was the matter with them, so I decided that here might be a good opportunity for me to make a little money, and maybe, too, I could contribute to his education, which he had thoroughly impressed upon me was generally expensive. I said, "Professor, if you are goin' to sell the mules, you might just as well sell 'em to me because I ain't got no more sense than to be able to tell what a mule is thinkin' about."

I bid him $100, which was $50 less than what he had paid for the team of mules. Well, I could tell right quick that this was cuttin' him deep, so I set in to explain to him that something you couldn't use wasn't worth anything to you and you had better get what you could out of it and apply it to something more suitable, such as a pair of good gentle horses.

He stomped around and kicked his toe in the dirt and took a clean white handkerchief out of his pocket and wiped around his head and collar and said after a good bit of silence that he would take $125 for the mules. I bid him $115, and after some more deep thought and considerable and brilliant conversation, he decided to take my offer of $115.

As I began to dig around in my pockets for the money— it was customary for traders in those days to carry a right smart of money—I told him that it would be better to use a different type of harness for horses and since that was new harness and had hardly been used and fit the mules good, that I would like to buy it too. He said that he always tried to have the best of everything and that I might not be interested in giving as much as the harness had cost. I told him that it might be more than I could afford, but how much did the harness cost? He added up the cost of the collar and the lines and so forth and it all came to $45, which would make the team and the harness cost $160. I counted him out the money, and he folded it up, put it in that white handkerchief, and stuck it in his shirt pocket and buttoned the flap.

I said, "Well, you'll want to drive back to the barn and take your cultivator, so I'll turn in at the gate and meet you up there, but before you start to the barn, if you don't mind, I'd like to change the harness a little on these mules. You couldn't make 'em drive any worse."

Well, when Professor Know-It-All bought this new harness and put these new lines on his team, his education in simple matters seemed to be a little short. The outside line on each mule or horse runs straight from the driver's hand through a ring on the hames at the collar and down to and fastens on the outside rings of the bits. Then the checkline that runs across from the outside over to the other mule and hooks onto the inside ring of the other mule's bits has to be attached to the long line with a buckle, making it adjustable, and by reason of the distance across the tongue of any implement or just because the mules have to be far enough apart to walk good, the checkline is much longer than the outside line.

Well, Professor Know-It-All had put these new lines on that new harness just backwards and the checkline was the outside line and the short line was the inside line and he was constantly pullin' the mules toward each other, which made them work on top of the bed—especially with their forefeet—instead of in two separate furrows on each side of the bed. And the only way that those mules could have ever made a turn at the end of a row was just to use their own sense in spite of the way Professor Know-It-All was pullin' them. He wasn't a big man and not overly stout in his arms, which had been developed openin' and shuttin' a book and usin' a pencil, so the mules had managed to survive this awful line arrangement.

As I took the lines off the harness and changed them on one mule to the other and hooked them up like they should be, I couldn't help but mention to Professor Know-It-All the value of havin' more common knowledge than a mule. When I had 'em rigged like they should be, I told him to go ahead and drive 'em to the barn and he might just as well plow a row back and I'd meet him at the barn.

By now, he had grown very silent and the sweat popping out on his brow wasn't exactly caused by the heat. I handed him the lines and he got on the seat of his cultivator and started the team. The nice little sorrel mare mules stepped over in each furrow that they belonged in and you could tell they were walkin' much relieved and relaxed from what they had been and were pullin' that cultivator and plowin' a beautiful straight row.

I struck a lope and turned in at the gate that led to the barn and watched him. When he got to the end of the row and should have turned to come to the barn, he turned back down another row. The little mules turned nicely at the turn row at the fence, and after about three more turns like this with me watchin' across the field from the barn, he finally drove up to the barn. He got up off his cultivator and laid the lines off to one side on the ground and said, "Ben, you have robbed me."

I said, "I hardly think so, Professor. However, I'm rather proud of my morning's work in buyin' that team of mules and harness."

He said, "I have seen what you did."

I said, "Yeah, I think it's got somethin' to do with the law of physics but I ain't smart enough to know."

By now, he was mad at himself and sick at the deal and said, "I'm going to give you your money back."

"No, Professor, that ain't my money but them mules and that harness do belong to me, and we just as well unhitch 'em from your cultivator so I can take 'em home."

He said, "Now let's talk this over. I originally gave $150 for this pair of mules and I see now that they are still worth it, so I'll give you $150 for them back."

"Well, Professor, I guess that will be all right, but you know education is time-consumin' and expensive and there ain't many of us have the advantage and opportunity to get smartened up and I believe I'll have to charge you $15 for teachin' you how to rig up the lines on that pair of mules."

Well, he slobbered and stomped considerably and gave me another lecture about neighborliness and takin' advantage of other people and I told him I understood all that but I thought he ought to consider the $15 tuition.

After he stood for a few minutes, he unwrapped the money so he could mop his sweat with that handkerchief. After he stood for a few more minutes and looked at the team and rubbed them on the head and straightened a wrinkle out of one of the lines, he said, "I'm going to pay you if you won't tell about this transaction and cause me further embarrass-ment."

I said, "Professor, I won't exactly make that promise. I'll just keep this in store until you begin to take advantage of a gatherin' of friends that just want to visit and that ain't in-terested in furtherin' their education every time you join the crowd."

He wrote a check for $50 and put it with the money and handed it to me without any of the nice comments like "Thank you" or "Come back to see me" that you would expect from an educated man, and I in my ignorant way said, "Much obliged," and stepped on my horse and rode on.

SADDLE
MARKS

The cavalry was buying some remount horses and had put out the word as to the dates when cavalry officers would be in certain Southwest Texas towns to inspect and buy horses. In the years past I had at different times sold the cavalry lots of horses, but it had been a good while since the government had actually been active in the horse market. Most horses of the type and quality that they wanted had been sell-

ing to polo buyers and to be used in rodeo sports that were beginning to be popular. Rodeo itself had started to be a profession rather than a holiday pastime for real working cowboys and ranch hands.

This recent cavalry demand was of course welcomed by horsemen. The cavalry officers had been to Abilene and had spent a couple of days inspecting and buying horses. News had traveled fast back through the cactus and mesquite that the cavalry officers were being extremely choosy, weren't overlooking any blemishes, and were being very hard about height, size, mouths, soundness, and colors, which to most horse traders meant that this was just a small fill-in or replacement order and a horse would have to be extra good to pass inspection, and the going price was $165 a head.

The next closest date that had been announced was an inspection at Brownwood, Texas, the next month. I made a fast trip down through Southwest Texas and talked to a good many local horsemen. Most of them knew about the cavalry order and in those days most horsemen knew whether or not they had a cavalry horse. There were a lot of half thoroughbred horses out of the native mares scattered through the ranch country that were good usin' horses, but very few of them would pass a rugged military inspection. There was not much slack in the price they would cost and the price they would bring if you had to move 'em very far and if you had one rejected on you, then it would be hard to make any money.

I spent the night in Del Rio, Texas, and talked horses in the lobby of the hotel with a few ranchers. Some of them said they had horses that would pass inspection but they couldn't stand to take the price. The next morning I crossed over into Old Mexico and was driving along about twenty-five miles from the border when I noticed a fair-sized band of what appeared at a glance to be top-quality horses that would do for the cavalry, so I turned down a rocky road to a prosperous-looking ranch headquarters and was met at the gate by a well-kept Mexican that spoke good English. He spread the usual amount of Mexican hospitality shown to a stranger from across the border that might be carrying United States money.

He invited me into a nicely kept patio and pretty soon some of the womenfolk spread the little table with some Mexican-corn-made snacks and brought out some cold water for our enjoyment, all of course with the intention of stimulating conversation. After a while I worked around to the subject of the horses in the trap pasture between the headquarters and the road. In the conversation I learned that there was a rich Mexican who owned the ranch and lived in San Antonio, Texas, and that my fat-faced, talkative entertainer was the ranch manager and he had the authority to sell the horses.

When he saw I was interested in buying some horses, he loosened up both ends of his tongue considerably and in good Mexican and fair English rattled off of both ends of it. He stood up and called loud to somebody back behind the house. A slender teen-age Mexican kid came running at his call. He was wearing a pair of spoke rowel spurs that weighed as much as his boots and made lots of noise on the Mexican tile. After a quick batch of palaver and hand waving, the young Mexican disappeared toward the corrals and my host turned to tell me that he would have those horses in the corral for me too look at *muy pronto*.

I watched as two young Mexicans rode around the horses and bunched them together and started them to the corrals. These were horses that had been brought in regularly and they bunched and headed for the corrals as though they were used every day. This was a band of good solid-colored horses with very few natural white markings and they had the nicest mouths that ever belonged to a bunch of horses. They were all five and six years old and when they were roped out as broncs none of their teeth had been broken or injured and the bars and gums were not damaged. From the front teeth and to the back teeth their mouths were soft and sensitive and had not been cut nor caloused with harsh bits, which was another unusual thing about five- and six-year-old Mexican horses. All the horses had white saddle marks on both sides of their backs that showed very plainly that they had had saddles on for long hours and hard rides. A few had white hairs behind the forelegs on their bodies where the cinch fits, not uncommon in a hot country where horses sweat and lather from the heat.

I walked around and walked up to a good many of these nicely broke horses and I asked if they rode and handled as good as they behaved when you were around them afoot. Of course, all this time the Mexican foreman had been explaining to me how good these horses were and how great the thoroughbred stallion was that was their papa and how much care had been given these fine horses. While he was telling me all this, I had the young cowboy saddle up a good brown horse. I noticed the cowboy stepped up in the saddle without untracking the horse, which is proof positive that a horse is well-broke to ride or else the cowboy is reckless. The horse galloped off good, changed leads, and made a figure eight just like he was in review at Fort Bliss.

While we were lookin' and talkin', the young cowboy rode six horses and all of them did as well as the first. It was in the hot afternoon and I thought it foolish to ride the rest of these gentle, saddle-marked, cinch-marked good horses. We had been talkin' about price in a casual sort of way, and as we had moved over to shade under a shed that was roofed with sotol and other cactus stalks, my not-too-dumb Mexican foreman was trying to bring out how much I could pay for the horses instead of how little he could take but neither of us was givin' out any hard dollar information. By late afternoon I decided that if I was going to buy the horses I had better do so because I wanted to cross back over the border before night and he had already agreed to deliver the horses at the border in about three days at whatever price we settled on.

The export and import duty at that time was $15 per head and I was figurin' that into the price of the horses. Then the transporation cost from the border to Brownwood would be something like $5 a head. I thought it would be nice if I could make a real killing on this bunch of horses and not have to be hunting single horses all over the Southwest and buying one at a time. Since this Mexican horse salesman wasn't too dumb, he pointed out that these horses would be worth more to me in a bunch than buying them one at a time.

When we had about run out of conversation and he saw I was going to leave and he would finally have to set the price on the horses, he told me he would take $100 a head and deliver the horses to the border and I would pay the money to the owner in San Antonio. Well, I had been involved in arrangements like these before and they weren't too hard to handle; the purpose of this kind of deal was to get the money out of Mexico without too much difficulty, and if I paid the money in the United States, it would be still a better deal for the San Antonio Mexican rancher.

When I started my car about an hour and half later, he hadn't decided to take the $75 that I had offered per head but suddenly he decided to take $80 per head and I made the trade with him. I said that I would call his boss in San Antonio and tell him of the trade and then his boss could send him word to deliver the horses to me at the border on whatever date we set in our final discussions.

I spent the night in Del Rio and called the ranch owner; he said he would meet me by noon the next day in Del Rio. He turned out to be a very smart Mexican ranch operator who had both American and Mexican citizenship and must have been past seventy years old and a horseman for a lifetime. The trade as I had discussed it with his foreman on thirty-two head of horses was agreeable with him and we sent word by a man—who I guess may have been considered a chauffeur or flunky—to the ranch foreman to have the horses at the border in three days.

The horses were the ones I had looked at and were in good condition. Several of them had been ridden on the trip. I went through the red tape and paid the duty and brought the horses across the bridge and penned them on this side at the railroad stock pens. We went back to the St. Regis Hotel, where I paid the old gentleman, and then he started back to San Antonio. Late that afternoon I loaded the horses out to be shipped to Brownwood. The railroad connections weren't direct and the horses were switched around on different tracks and got to Brownwood two days later in fair condition.

The next day was the day set for horse inspection and I had gotten to Brownwood in time to hire some cowboys to help me show these horses. The old Brownwood Horse and Mule Barns were crowded with prospective cavalry horses from all over the surrounding country, and since the receiving Army officers had only set one day for Brownwood, it was going to be a day of hard, fast inspections and since they had so many horses to pick from, they weren't gonna take anything that didn't suit them.

The next morning it didn't take long to get rid of the three- and four-year-old horses, which were actually a little young. Then it didn't take very much eyeballin' inspection to cut out the coarser and heavier horses that were too big and the ones that were too small, and by noon they were looking hard at what they would buy. Cowboys were saddling and unsaddling and riding horses between two colonels that were standing about three hundred yards apart. As you rode toward one of them, he caught the horse's way of travel and as you rode back away from him, he looked for blemishes, the same as the colonel at the other end of the line was doing. They called for walking, trotting, galloping, and reining, and especially figure eights. A horse with a hard mouth or too light a mouth was waved out pretty fast. Almost sundown it dawned on the colonels that they didn't have as many horses as they were intending to buy and coming up next were my thirty-two head.

The two young cowboys that I had hired to help show my horses were naturally catchin' out those that showed a little dried saddle sweat; these were the ones that had been ridden to deliver the herd. I rode two and each one of them rode two and we showed them one right after another and the colonels took all six of these horses in a row. It was nearly sundown and these horses had shown so perfectly that they looked at the rest of 'em at the halter. We led and trotted 'em with the horses we had shown and they gave me a voucher, which was the way they paid you, for thirty head of horses; they rejected two on size.

I stayed in town that night and the talk around the Brownwood Hotel lobby among the cowboys and horsemen was of me gettin' thirty head sold and only two rejected, and they wondered how I ever found that many good, sound, uniform horses five and six years old. John Yantis at the bank, whom I knew well, cashed my government voucher the next morning and then I left town.

That fall the government put out another order for some horses, the cavalry inspection to be at the remount station at San Angelo, Texas. I had six horses that I knew were sound, typy, and well schooled and that the remount officers would love at first sight. I thought that they were so good that they might wind up as officers' mounts, so I was on hand early the morning of inspection. Colonel Voorhies came down the line looking at horses and when he saw me he stopped in his tracks. He went into the damnedest fit that I ever saw a military individual have. He wanted to know how I got saddle marks on twenty-four head of horses that had never been rode. He said they crippled half of his sergeants and stable hands and that six of them never were broken and were disposed of in order to keep from killing off the rest of the soldiers in the remount station.

He got this off his chest with an abundance of profanity very expertly blended into the declaration, and I was at a loss to know what was the matter because all the horses we rode had been exceptionally well mannered. When I said, "I've got six horses to show you here now," he ordered me off the grounds with my horses and said he hoped that from then on I would sell horses to the enemy. He said I would be performing a great patriotic service for my country and there was no doubt that if I furnished the enemy all their horses, we would win the war without a battle.

This was a pretty bad blow to a horse trader that thought he had a good reputation with the remount buyers and I was at a complete loss to know what the problem was. I saw him again at dinner and he threw another fit and called across the dining room. An old gray-headed crippled-up sergeant came hobbling across to where we were and the colonel introduced me as the man that broke up the remount station last summer.

This didn't make me feel any better but this old sergeant had lived with more bad horses than the colonel had and wanted to visit with me about the horses because he knew, the same as I, that he might face another bunch like them sometime. So we sat down in the corner of the lobby. He told me how rank those horses were with a man on them and how gentle they handled around the post. He said he couldn't figure it out. I didn't shed any light on this deal by telling them that I got these horses in Old Mexico, but for at least a while my government horse business had balked.

Early that fall while it was still hot and dry and dusty, I had an order from some fellows in Kansas for some big, big steers. By reason of the type and quality of cattle that the order called for and due to the difference in price, I again crossed the border at Del Rio to try to buy some big Mexican steers. I was driving along that same road and as I passed that Mexican headquarters where I bought the bad horses, I still wondered what they did to me but I didn't intend to stop and ask.

A few miles down the road I saw a bunch of horses wearing old-timey, big-horned Mexican saddles and some had as many as three heavy woven saddle blankets on and all the saddles were double-cinched and the horses were just wearin' hackamores without any lead rope on them. There was a small Mexican kid, maybe twelve or thirteen years old, driving this bunch of horses down the fence line in a long lope. They were wringing wet with sweat and lather working out from under the cinches and saddles, and I drove along the road behind real slow to see what was going on. As these horses came to a big earthen pool, they stopped and lined up around the pool to drink. As they left the water, they shaded up in some mesquite trees and some of 'em started to roll with their saddles on. Then I noticed that some of these saddles didn't even have stirrups on 'em. This Mexican kid watered his horse and rode up in the shade.

I stopped my car and crawled through the fence but before I got far I turned back to the car and got a big jug full of ice water. Well, I talked to the Mexican kid awhile. We made signs and he talked some English and that ice water made a big hit with him and we got real friendly. I told him about how it was north of the border and he listened.

It was awful hot in that Mexican sunlight and before my ice water ran out, I asked him where he was taking the horses and he said "Nowhere" in Mexican and waved his hands and finally explained to me that he was just taking them around and around that pasture. I said, "Why have you got saddles on 'em?" And in broken English with a big grin on his face and waving both hands, he said that he run the horses and get them real hot to where the blankets and the saddles will make white spots come on their backs and on their sides and some damn silly gringo will come by and buy them for broke.

FENCE
TROUBLE

As early as I can remember, Joe D. Hughes of Houston was the biggest contractor in Texas or maybe in the world that moved dirt to build railroad beds, whether it be dirt fills or excavation. Then he moved on into building the early-day roadbeds and highways when teams and horse-drawn equipment was still used. As the oil industry developed, Joe D. Hughes moved into the oil fields with his teams to do the dirt excavation for slush pits, the building of roads and the movement of oil well machinery, and later on to build pipelines. This was at a time when almost all dirt movement was with teams. Joe D. Hughes would buy a carload of big, stout, sound mules anytime, and it was said that he once had fifteen hundred teams working at dirt movement in Texas at one time.

At breakfast one morning before daylight in the old Stockyards Hotel at Fort Worth, he told me that he especially needed some great big mules—sixteen hands and over and as heavy as he could get 'em—and if I knew where there was even one team, he would be back the following Monday and take time to look at 'em.

Mules seldom got this big and I knew they would be hard to find. I wasn't much more than a kid in the horse and mule business and it was pretty big of Old Man Hughes to take time to trade with me on what few head I usually had. However, he had always been a good buyer and was always encouragin' me, I guess because I was a kid. I told him I would have one pair for him to look at when he came back next week.

I knew a man on the Clear Fork of the Trinity River about twenty miles west of Fort Worth that had a pair of seal-brown horse mules as big as Joe D. Hughes had described or would ever want, so I saddled up early next morning and rode into this fellow's feed lot a little after dinnertime.

This pair of mules could jump any kind of a fence, but he didn't know that I knew it. He fed steers and also kept a bunch of young mules on feed, but this pair of big mules that he worked to the feed wagon could be in any lot they wanted to. They might be together or they might be separated because they could stand flat-footed and jump any fence he had. This, of course, he intended to keep a secret from me.

He was in the feed barn mixin' feed to be put out that afternoon. After we visited a little while, he knew I hadn't rode twenty miles to ask about his health and asked, "Ben, what didya come after?"

I described the pair of horse mules I wanted just like I didn't know he had any, and he said, "I've got the very team for ya."

Well, he didn't know which fence they had jumped last, and he said, "Well, I don't know where the boys turned 'em when they unhitched 'em at dinner, but they're in one of the pens here in the feed yard."

I left my horse standin' tied outside and we walked through the alley until he spotted them in one of the corrals eatin' out of a trough with the cattle. He hastened to explain that he had rather turn a work team in with a pen of cattle because they were so much easier to catch than turn them in with the other mules.

We walked into the feed yard and I held the gate open while he drove the mules into the alley. Oddly enough, they let him walk up to 'em and put halters on 'em without tryin' to jump another fence. They were six or seven years old, full brothers, and, of course, perfectly matched, no scars or blemishes, with just a little white hair in the manes where their collars worked, which proved that they were sure enough work mules.

He didn't price 'em too high because there weren't a lot of buyers for that kind of mule, and I knew by the grapevine that he was tired of wonderin' where they were because of their jumpin' habits, so I decided to contest him about the price. He had asked $350 for the team and, of course, I immediately took off $50 and offered $300. All the while I was askin' various questions about the mules' habits and disposition, and finally I asked him, "Ed, will these mules stay in a fence of any kind or do they have to be in high fences like you've got here in the feed yard?"

He assured me in firm tones that I need not have any fear, that a one-wire fence would hold 'em just as good as a fence five wires high. I took him at his word and he finally took $325 for the mules and in the deal furnished me halters and rope to put on 'em. By middle of the afternoon I had started back to Fort Worth leadin' the fine big pair of sure-'nuff-Joe-D.-Hughes-kind-of-mules.

I knew what I had, so I took them to the Burnett-Yount Horse and Mule Barn in Fort Worth and put the two in a big double stall where there would be no possibility of them gettin' away. I didn't enter this pair in Monday's auction and sure enough, Mr. Hughes came by and gave me $400 for the pair. This was late fall and the mule business was good all season.

In the late spring I was drivin' a herd of horses and mules up the Clear Fork Road toward Weatherford when I met the man that had sold me the big mules. He had started to Aledo but said he would have time to turn around and go back to his place, which was only three or four miles, if I wanted to sell him a pair of little, hard-twisted, sandy-land-type mules that he had picked out while we held them in the road.

We talked a good deal about the price of this pair of

smooth-mouthed mules, but they weren't worth a lot of money. He said he needed a light team for that summer to build fence with, and after enough horse traders' conversation to where neither one of us felt we had been too easy to do business with, he gave me $175 for this pair of little mules.

Several times in our conversation he had asked me, "Will these little mules jump fence?"

Of course, I knew he had a guilty conscious about that pair of big mules he had sold me, but their bad habit hadn't cost me any trouble at all. I had never let on that I knew they were a jumpin' pair of mules, and each time I answered him, I told him I would guarantee 'em not to jump a fence. He was about to write out a check when we came even with the lane that turned up to his place, and he asked me again in dead earnest, "Ben, you know these little mules won't jump?"

I said, "Ed, all mules have some kind of bad habit and I'm not sure whatever else might be the matter with 'em, but if they jump a fence, I'll give 'em to you."

That seemed to settle the argument and he took his little mules on up to his house and I drifted my herd on toward Weatherford.

He sent this pair of little mules to the back side of the ranch where there was a barn and some wire-fence corrals, and a man to start work buildin' fence. The next morning they found the little mules out in a big pasture and had considerable trouble gettin' 'em back in the corral. Three or four days later, they were in a neighbor's pasture and Ed had to send two men to catch 'em and bring 'em home. They were out and gone again the next week and Ed came to town after his money.

I said, "Ed, this is goin' to disappoint you, but I don't believe the little mules jumped the fence."

He went into a fair tantrum and told me that when mules got out three or four times in a week they'd have to be fence-jumpers. I asked him where they were then, and he said that best he knew they were in the corral at the fencer's camp, but he didn't know how long they'd be there. He wanted me to go out with him, so he could prove to me that they were jumpin' fence. I hesitated to go with him, but he said he would bring me straight back to town.

As we got in sight of the wire corral, it was late afternoon and the little mules had just finished eatin' their oats for supper. As we drove up, one of them stuck his head under the wire fence where one wire was loose at the bottom, dropped down on his knees, and crawled through to the outside where the grass was greener. He turned around and made a little mule conversation and the other little mule came to the same spot and dropped down on his knees, stuck his head under the loose bottom wire, and crawled out.

Ed nearly swallowed his teeth and started to turn red in the face and cuss and I said, "The agreement was if they jumped the fence, I'd give you your money back. It's gettin' late, so take me back to town. You know you don't want me to spend the night with you in the humor that you're in."

FOREIGN
TRADE

It was late spring and the horse and mule business was about to taper off for the summer. The farmers had already bought whatever fresh teams they needed to start their year's work of making a crop and it was a natural thing for the major portion of the horse and mule business to slack off until fall. However, a trader would have some business all summer on riding horses of various kinds. It was too early in the year for the cattle in the country to be fat enough to be slicked off, and, being a trader, I was goin' to have trouble stayin' in business the next thirty or forty days until the summer cow business started.

I had brought my last little bunch of work mules in to the Fort Worth Horse and Mule Market on Sunday and went over to the Texas Hotel in the main part of Fort Worth and spent the night.

The next morning when I got on the elevator to come down to the lobby, there were two handsome young men dressed in foreign military uniforms and I could tell at a glance by their hard-top boots, their little legged britches, and knob spurs that they belonged to some country's cavalry. As I gave 'em the once-over, the blond, light-complexioned one smiled and said in a foreign brogue, "You look the part of a cowboy."

I said, "Well, I hope so. If I didn't, I'd be counterfeit because I'm sure not anything else."

It was early in the morning and I felt good and thought I would be nice to foreigners and said, "You look the part of a general."

They both laughed about the "general" part, and, of course, I knew so little about military uniforms that so far as I was concerned, they may have been generals.

When we left the elevator and started across the lobby toward the dining room, I said, "You generals just as well have breakfast with me. It's not often that I get to associate with such military personalities."

We went in and picked out a table, and as we were about to sit down, they introduced themselves. One was a captain and the other a colonel in the Italian cavalry. As the morning breakfast progressed, they told me they were in America to buy pack mules for the Italian army. Well, my conversation brightened up considerably because of that little bunch of mules that I had in that morning's sale.

We had a big visit and they asked me quite a bit about the Texas mule market. Of course, I didn't run it down none and asked if they would care to see my mules before the auction started. They thought that that would be fine, and since they didn't know their way around much and neither of us had cars, I turned guide for them and took 'em on the right streetcar to get us to North Fort Worth.

We went to Ross Bros. Horse and Mule Barn where the sale was to be held that particular Monday and Tuesday.

Wad Ross and C. B. Teems and other horse and mule dealers rushed out to greet the "Generals" and tell them they
were expectin' them and all that stuff, and these military
gentlemen gently brushed them off and followed me on down
to look at my mules.

Denny, the barn foreman, came up and offered to help
show my mules and we turned them out one at a time on
the plank alley for the Italians to inspect. By now we had
gotten real friendly and I was callin' them Capitan and
Colonel and they were callin' me by my first name or sometimes Cowboy. They told me that twelve of my twenty
mules would sure pass their inspection and they would bid
on them.

I asked how long they were goin' to be in the mule market
in Texas and the Colonel spoke up and said it might take
several weeks to fill their needs. They just didn't know how
many of the right kind of mules would be coming to the
Fort Worth market. I explained to them that since I knew
now the type of mules they wanted I probably could bring in
as many as a carload or more of the right kind the next week.
They encouraged me to go buy whatever mules I thought
would pass their inspection—but the mules had to be halter-
broke to lead and handle, but they didn't have to be broke
to work or ride.

They were rather busy during the auction, and, of course,
all the mule dealers around were tryin' to get to them one way
or another. Wad Ross and Parker Jamison had taken them
in hand so that nobody else could talk to them. They were
good bidders on my mules and the ones they didn't bid on
sold way too cheap.

Late that afternoon I got a chance to tell them that I
would be back next week with some mules for them to send
to Italy. I saddled old Charlie and rode out about dark.
Charlie was a good road horse with a long, head-noddin',
swingin' fox trot, and after I crossed the Clear Fork of the
Trinity on the Old White Settlement Road where there was

very little traffic, I dozed off to sleep. Charlie pawed on the barn gate at home about midnight to wake me up.

I knew where there were some mules up about Graham and Graford northwest of home so I saddled old Beauty the next morning and led Charlie. You nearly always needed two horses on these long rides if you bought any stock to handle.

It took me several days to ride up to the country around Graham where I knew there had been some good young mules—and I was hopin' they were still there. Graham Stewart, who was a good rancher and especially a steer operator, had thirty-four head of mules on his ranch that in his terms were gettin' in his way, and he wanted to sell 'em. I think he had gathered these mules up as payment on some paper and maybe had bought a few of 'em; but I don't believe he had raised any of 'em. In spite of this, they were a pretty uniform set of mules.

He asked me $135 a head for these four- and five-year-old mules—and that was a little high for unbroke mules if the market had been active, but this late in the year, it was a whole lot too high. I told him that the mule business was nearly over and that the mules would need to be halter-broke, their manes roached and their tails sheared before they could be led into the auction ring, but I didn't fill him in that there were some Italian buyers in the country.

After a whole lot of conversation and a big ranch dinner, I bought the thirty-four head for $90 a head and turned them in the road and started home by way of Graham to Graford. At Graford I bought a few more and another one or two along the way and got into Weatherford with forty-seven head of mules that were just what the Italians needed to pack around in the mountains of their native land.

I had been gone for over a week and had missed one sale day at Fort Worth. In the late afternoon, I penned these fat, unbroke mules in the wagonyard and some of the local mule dealers asked me what I was goin' to do with 'em— that there wasn't any market for mules from now on through the summer and I would have plenty of time to get them broke for the fall trade. I told them that I had planned on dressin' 'em up and takin' 'em in to Forth Worth for the Italians. Silas Kemp spoke up and said, "The Italians got their boat loaded with more mules than you can shake a stick at and I think they've already shipped out."

Well, since it was that season of the year when there weren't any buyers comin' to the market from Tennessee, Mississippi, and Alabama, the Italians hadn't been havin' any trouble buyin' mules that passed their inspection, and I realized that Silas could be tellin' me the truth.

I remembered that the Captain's name was Spiro, so I eased up to the Texas Café, got in the pay phone booth, and closed the door real tight so the loafers couldn't hear, then put in a call to him. When I got him on the phone, I explained why I had missed the sale the week before. I painted him a picture of how good my mules were and said I'd try to get into Fort Worth the comin' sale day. He explained that they had nearly all the mules they wanted but if mine were as good as I said that they were, they would wait to see them before they finished their order. Well, I thanked him and promised him I would have the mules in there for sure Sunday afternoon for the Monday sale. It was Wednesday and the job of halter-breakin' forty-seven head of mules to lead by Saturday night was something I hadn't figured on.

When you rope a wild mule around the neck, you cause the lariat rope to be pulling down on the heavy muscular part of his neck. If he gets his head away from you and his hind quarters to you, he will pull a good horse half to death and a man afoot just can't begin to hold him. Now, if you can manage to get him to turn his head to you and make him back up from you, the rope will slip up behind his ears and around his throat to where you can choke him down. When he hits the ground, you give him slack and put a halter on his head before he can get up.

Experience will teach you to dread ropin' mules by the

head and neck. I thought the smart way to do this would be to have a man help me cut off one mule at a time, then run him up past me in the hallway of the barn where I would rope him by the forefeet instead of the head. When the mule would hit the end of the rope with a lot of power, he'd throw himself and this would be very educational to him and easier on me.

The hallway of this barn was floored with 4 x 12 oak lumber that was well worn and had sort of a fuzzy-like finish to it from the wear of horses' and mules' feet. After I had put a halter on a mule and let him up, Cat Medford, an old-time trader, leaned on the fence and said, "Benny, let me tell you somethin'."

Well, it wasn't hard to get me to listen—if he knew anything—to get these mules gentle enough to show the Italians by Sunday, and he said, "If you'll wet that plank floor real good, a runnin' mule can't stand up too good and you can bust him on that floor with a lot less effort. Don't try to halter 'em the first time. Run 'em up and down this alley and forefeet 'em several times, and before you know it, when that rope hits their legs, instead of runnin' they'll stop and freeze in their tracks and you can walk up to 'em and halter 'em standin' up."

He had told me this in a low tone of voice because there were a few people up and down the hall of the barn watchin' the show. I rigged up a hose to the hydrant over a water trough and soaked that oakwood floor good. I decided it might be a little hard for me with my high-heel boots to stand up on that slick floor when I was jerkin' the forefeet out from under a mule, so I took a big four-strand silk manilla lariat rope and tied it around a big post about the middle of the hall of the barn. This way when that runnin' mule passed me and I roped it, I'd just jiggle the slack until the mule hit the end of the rope and busted himself on that wet floor.

I worked about half of these mules through that morning

and decided I would see if it was goin' to work on 'em before I broke the other half the first time. So that afternoon I forefooted them a couple of more times, and about the fourth or fifth time around, when that rope hit their forefeet, those wild mules came to a slidin' stop. They had rollers in their noses and things on their minds and they might stomp the floor a little like they wanted to paw you, but the idea of fallin' kept them standin' still while I walked up and slipped a halter on them.

During the time I had been ropin' these mules, every time I caught one I hollered "Whoa" in a loud, firm voice, and it had gotten to where when a rope touched their forelegs and I hollered "Whoa" they would get the message and stand still. By Friday night I had a hall full of wild mules that I could walk up to and holler "Whoa" and put a halter on.

On Saturday I got a couple of stout-wristed farm boys to help me and we roached their manes and sheared their tails, and, believe it or not, they were a dressed-up bunch of good-lookin' mules from four to five years old and weighed from 950 to 1050 pounds, which was ideal size for Italian pack mules.

Sunday morning I got some town cowboys to help me get the mules to the White Settlement Road and turned them out about daylight. I drove them the rest of the way to Fort Worth by myself with little or no trouble. They were all wearin' halters and draggin' halter ropes and steppin' on them, which was pullin' on their heads and makin' their noses a little sensitive. I drove the thirty miles into the Fort Worth Horse and Mule Market a little before dark. I got Pete Shelton to help me get the halters off of them and we turned them into one of those nice big square pens with lots of good hay and shell corn and oats. I put my saddle horses in a pen out from under the roofed part of the Horse and Mule Market and left them well cared for. Then I got on the streetcar and went to the main part of Fort Worth.

Sure enough, I found my Italian Captain and Colonel at

the hotel havin' what they called dinner but it was supper to me. We visited and I told them about my good mules and they said they only needed sixty more mules.

When the sale started the next morning and the barn hands went to halterin' my mules so they could lead them into the auction ring, I decided it would be best for me to go up to the auction stand and watch them come in the ring. The Italians bought forty-three head, and four sold too cheap to other buyers. Since these mules were broke only enough to be haltered and had never been tied hard and fast, I never knew whether or not they wrecked the ship at sea.

THE
LAST
TRAIL DRIVE
THROUGH
DOWNTOWN
DALLAS

I was riding past Hamilton's filling station and garage on a pretty good sixty-dollar horse when a fellow that was buying gas hollered at me and waved me to come over. I wasn't in a big hurry, so I reined over to the side of the road and he walked out from the station and asked, "What will you take for that horse?"

Well, that was a question I wasn't bad to answer and I wasn't riding one of my favorites. In order to leave some room for him to trade I said, "Seventy-five dollars."

He said, "I really don't want to buy no horses. I was just wondering what one

like that would be worth in this part of the country, because there was a man that tried to sell me some at Paint Rock, Texas, that were pretty nice lookin' horses about the size of this one for $10 a head."

I said, "I don't know where Paint Rock is, but if you can buy horses like this one for $10 a head, it will have to be a long way to keep me from goin' after 'em."

He said, "Well, it's too far to go horseback. It's about two hundred and fifty miles southwest of here down close to San Angelo."

I asked, "Who's the man? That don't sound too far."

He told me that Shultz Bros. and some other ranchers had a good many young unbroken horses for sale. By this time Hamilton had tended to his car and had made me very miserable with that piece of information, and I waved at him and rode off.

It was early summer and I had been out of school for about two weeks and was pretty well caught up with my loafin' and visitin' and kind of needed some place to go after a bunch of horses. I talked it over with my dad late that evening about them cheap horses out in West Texas and that I had all summer to go get 'em, break 'em, and sell 'em. I thought I would be less trouble to him if I was gone for two or three months.

He didn't see much wrong with that and he knew I had several hundred dollars of tradin' money, so he told me to rig up and leave when I got ready but be back in time to start to school that fall. He said he wanted to hear from me once in a while so he would know that the rest of the horse traders hadn't gotten all my money and I hadn't starved to death.

That night I got a map and figured out where Paint Rock was and how to get there by common roads and highways ahorseback. I wasn't worried too much if this particular bunch of horses had been sold, because if horses sold that cheap, they must be plenty more in the same country.

Next morning I rigged up Beauty and led Charlie with a light pack on him, mostly just a bedroll and some extra clothes. It was a nice time of year, the grass was green along the roads and the running water was clean in the creeks that crossed the roads and highways and the nights were always nice and cool. I did get rained on a few times during the trip, but there wasn't much danger of me meltin' and there was no other reason that a good rain would hurt a young cowboy.

About ten nights later I camped in the wagonyard at Ballinger and ate supper at an old-timey two-story concrete block hotel over by the railroad. Settin' on the porch of the hotel after supper that night. I got into a conversation with some railroad men and two or three native merchants and began to ask questions about the horses and ranches.

The country around Ballinger was mostly farms, but I had already crossed lots of grassland and the farms were along the Colorado River and plenty of ranches lay beyond there. These old native merchants said that if I wanted to buy horses I had better not say it very loud or I'd get more than I could handle.

The next morning the wagonyard man told me that it was about twenty miles to Paint Rock. He said that anybody there could tell me how to find the Shultz Ranch or the Paint Rock Cattle Company, which was the two names that I had. I rode into Paint Rock a little after dinner and an old country mercantile man told me that the Shultz Ranch had a phone and before I rode out there, why didn't I call 'em. Well, I was just a big green country boy and hadn't learned to cut off much mileage by usin' the telephone and writin' letters.

He got the Shultz Ranch on the phone for me and talked to the foreman; he told him that there was a kid that wanted to buy some horses. As he stepped back from the phone, he said, "Here, you talk to him."

The old man had said I was a kid and I guess my conversation sounded like it too, so the foreman wasn't too much impressed and evidently didn't think he had much of a horse buyer because he said he would come in and talk to me that afternoon when he had finished working on the windmill.

I bought up a batch of cold grub and ate it off the counter at the mercantile. It was the heat of the day and business wasn't too rushin', so the old man and me had a good visit. After he found out where I was from, he said it looked like I came a long way to get eight or ten horses. He was talkin' to me like I was a kid and I thought I was grown but he probably didn't think I had enough money to pay for more than eight or ten horses and then they would have to be cheap.

There was some shade trees around the mercantile and a good place to graze my horses, so I slipped the bits out of their mouths where they could drag the reins and graze till they was full, and I stretched out under the lacy shade of a mesquite tree and went to sleep. I waked up after a while and made it back to the mercantile and got me some candy and a cold drink for a wake-up tonic.

It was a long, draggy afternoon and it was real late when this foreman drove up in a pickup and walked out to where I was shadin' under a tree with my horses and asked, "Are you that kid that called about buyin' some horses?"

He was a big, stout, ranchy-lookin' fellow about forty years old, and I guess he had a right to call me a kid, but I thought horse buyers ought to be treated with a little more respect, so I said, "Yeah, are you the flunky of the outfit that's got 'em for sale?"

He started to bristle a little bit but then he decided it was funny. As he looked at the sucker rod windmill stains on his clothes and hands, he said, "Yeah, I guess you would call me that."

We talked on and he said that he didn't believe that he had time to round up these horses just to sell three or four head.

"Well," I said, "you think like a flunky too. How many head you got?"

He went to tryin' to figure up and count on his fingers, talkin' about thirty head of four-year-olds and a few threes and some older horses. He finally squinted one eye and looked up at the sun and said he guessed it would be about a hundred and thirty head of horses.

I asked, "What's the askin' price?"

He said that he had been told to get $10 a head for them straight across and I asked, "Will you round 'em up if you could sell half of 'em?"

He said, "We got so many horses and grass is gettin' short in the horse pasture that we'll round them up to sell less than that. But how do I know you got any money? You're just a kid."

I said, "How do I know you got any horses? You're just a flunky."

We was gettin' pretty well acquainted by now and he said, "Why don't we drive out there in the pickup and see some of them before dark and then you'll know whether you're interested or not."

I said, "That's a good idea, only it's a poor way to buy horses."

He said, "Well, we could round them up tomorrow morning if you think you would buy enough of them to make it worthwhile."

Since I was goin' to be gone for a little while, I tied my horses up like they ought to be to wait on me and we drove out to the ranch. I opened several gates while he did the driving and we went into a pasture that was fairly open, with only some scattered mesquite trees and big rocks in the way. We drove around close to several small bunches of horses that had just left the shade and began to graze in the late afternoon. I didn't see a horse that wasn't worth more than $10 and I thought a lot of them were worth $50 if I could

move them far enough east—and break 'em on the way—
where horses weren't quite so plentiful and there were more
people to use 'em.

It was dark when we got back to town and I guess my
conversation had convinced him that I could buy some
horses even if I was a kid. He told me he would have the
horses in the corral by middle of the next morning. I told
him that was plenty of time to ride out there. And we said
our good-byes.

I made camp under the big mesquite tree and took some
of the feed that I had tied on the back of my pack horse,
fed my horses, and staked them out to graze for the night.

I broke camp before daylight and packed my riggin' on
Charlie and saddled old Beauty and started for the ranch. I
got there way ahead of the horse herd and was settin' on
the fence when they came into sight and watched the cowboys bring them into the corral. This was a very colorful
bunch of West Texas ranch horses. They were from three
to seven years old, but most of them were fours and fives,
mares and geldings, unbroken and would weigh from 850
to 1,000 pounds. They were bay, roan, grey, and the chestnut horses had lots of splashy white markings on their faces
and legs. There was twelve head of old, fat cow horses that
had been turned out for one reason or another and they
would do to ride while moving the herd. There were six
little hard, fat mules, but I wouldn't describe them as being
"wore out" because nobody can quite tell by lookin' when a
mule is wore out.

There were no brood mares nor colts in the bunch, but I
did want to cut out enough horses to have just a hundred
head and I still hadn't agreed to give $10 for 'em, so we had
a whole lot of smart conservation for each other while we
was tryin' to make the trade. I offered him $5 a head and
take 'em all or $6 a head and cut out thirty.

Well, he acted like this made him mad enough to fight,
and after he had slobbered and stomped in the dirt and

jerked his horse a time or two, I said, "Well, I guess you were sure enough right about me wastin' your time."

He finally said he would take $10 a head for a hundred head or he would take $7 a head for all of 'em. We argued a little while longer and I pointed out ten head to him that were crippled one way or another that wouldn't "road" good and told him that if he would cut out that ten head I would give $7 a head for the rest of 'em.

I could tell that he thought he had cheated me to death and was real proud of himself and was going to be glad to tell his boss about robbin' a kid, but he sobered up a little bit to ask who was I going to give the check on and what town the bank was in. I got off the fence, turned around, and unbuckled the flap on my saddle pocket and pulled out a couple of brown paper sacks full of peanuts and candy and stuff. From down in the bottom I pulled out a wad of money that pretty near made this old boy faint and gave him forty-two twenty-dollar bills—$840 for a hundred and twenty head.

In the trade I had made with him he agreed to furnish two hands to help me get the horses to Ballinger, and as I was about to pay him, I reminded him again of this part of the trade and he said, "That's all right. With as many horses as you're buying, I might go along to help you."

We cut out the ten head that I didn't want and turned the rest out of the corral and drove them through the pasture to the public road. I turned Charlie loose with his pack to travel with the main herd while I rode Beauty on the drive. These horses were fresh and fat and traveled fast and we drove them to Ballinger and turned them into the wagonyard by late afternoon.

I took the two hands that the ranch had sent to help me and we went to a country café and ate up so much stuff that the kitchen might have run out of grease. They rode back to the ranch that night.

In those days in a West Texas town a hundred and

twenty head of horses didn't create much disturbance and not many people passing the wagonyard stopped to look at what I had. The next morning I told the old wagonyard man that I wanted to hire some help to drive these horses to East Texas. He said, "Kid, you need more than help. Let me sell you this little spring wagon over here by the fence. It used to be a grocery-store delivery wagon and it's in real good shape and I've got harness that will fit a pair of them little mules, and I know an old camp cook that you can hire to drive that wagon and keep camp for you all summer, if you want him that long."

There were times when I admitted to myself that I was pretty young. I really hadn't thought about a camp wagon and didn't see anything wrong with two or three pack horses driving along with the herd. But the camp wagon kind of appealed to me if somebody else was goin' to drive it. After walkin' around and shakin' the wheels and lookin' at the bed, I told him that if he could furnish that camp cook like he said he could, then we might make a deal on the wagon and harness.

I walked off uptown to eat some breakfast and when I got back to the wagonyard, there was a little old friendly Mexican that had a straggly beard that was almost white and I could tell had spent his early life cowboy'n and was spendin' his time now keepin' camp. I bought the spring wagon and harness enough for a team of mules from the old wagonyard man for $25. I made a trade with Old Friole for $2 a day to go with me and follow this bunch of horses until I sold out.

He thought this would be a real good job, and while we were leanin' on the corral fence lookin' at the horses and him pickin' out the pair of mules that he thought he ought to drive, he told me of an Indian boy that was originally from Oklahoma that sure did want to go home, and since I was going that way he thought I could hire the boy to help with the horses and the three of us would make a pretty good crew. I told Old Friole to put out the smoke signals and get his Indian boy—I was ready to deal with him.

He came back in about thirty minutes with what turned out to be a half-breed Choctaw Indian about twenty-three years old, a good cowboy, good-natured, and a good hand. He said, "I'll do twice as much work as Friole." Then he started politickin' and said, "Nearly as much as you, and I think I ought to have $2.50 a day."

I told him he didn't have as many years and as much brain as Old Friole. That made the old man laugh. Then I told him he didn't have as many horses as me so I would pay him $2 like I would Friole. He laughed pretty big and reset his hat and said I couldn't blame him for tryin' and he would be glad to have the job.

Me and Old Friole spent the rest of the day around the hardware and grocery stores gettin' some wagon bows and wagon sheets and iron skillets and Dutch ovens and other stuff that we would need for a camp. Choctaw helped Friole rig up the wagon bows and the wagon sheet and went to get his saddle and a small bag of clothes and a blanket.

By the next morning we had a new camp outfit and I had unpacked Charlie and threw all my riggin' in the wagon and Choctaw had started out by riding one of the old gentle horses. I paid the wagonyard man for feed and camp and we left town about ten o'clock for our first day on the road.

Unbroken horses drive a lot better down a road than gentle horses because they are sufficiently afraid of things not to be turning off and they haven't learned to turn down side roads to hunt for open gates the way gentle horses will do. There were plenty of young horses that took the lead and the gentler old horses and mules were mixed up in the herd and by the time we were four or five miles out of town, they had all settled down to walkin' and grazin' along the side of the road and it seemed that we had started out on a carefree horse drive that would end wherever we ran out of horses, which would probably be several hundred miles further and several months later.

Choc changed horses two or three times that day and none of the old horses showed any sign of being shod and were really pretty good mounts since they were fat and fresh. My personal horses were shod, but I didn't think we would shoe any of the others—we would just ride and drive and change them as soon as they showed signs of being tenderfooted.

We camped that night on the creek close to Talpa and I told Choc that we needed to start catchin' some of these older unbroke horses and let them drag a lead rope tied to a halter for a day. As they stepped on the lead rope in travelin', they would jerk and pull themselves until they got the tops of their heads and noses sore. Then when we started to ridin' them, they wouldn't pull on us as hard and we would be able to do a better job of holdin' them up and keepin' them from buckin'.

Choc was bigger and tougher than me and could do a better job of holdin' a bad horse's head up to where he couldn't buck, but anybody knows to cheat a big stout unbroke horse any way you can withont hurtin' him and when you think about breaking about a hundred head of 'em, you sure do want to go to saving your arms and legs and all the hide you can.

We made camp a little early, so we rigged out four extra halters, using all the extra rope we had besides our lariat ropes. While Friole was fixin' supper, I told Choc that while me and him was both pretty fresh on this drive, we had better catch some of those bigger horses and he thought that was all right too.

I eased around among the horses on Beauty, and without spinnin' my rope in the air, I sneakingly pitched it on one of the bigger bay horses that I was guessin' to be about five years old. As I eased the slack out of the rope and it took up

around his throat, he came undone and bawled like nothin'
—but a scared horse will bawl—ran to the end of the rope,
and went to pullin' back until he choked down.

Choc had been showing signs of being a good hand in the
little time we had been on the road and, sure enough, when
that old pony gave out of air and lunged forward and hit the
ground, Choc covered his head like a settin' hen, and when
they got up the big bay had a halter on. On the side of the
hill in the glade where we were camping there was a big
rock that I didn't think the bay could run off with, so me and
Choc wrapped the halter rope around this rock and tied it
so it couldn't come loose.

When staking an unbroke horse for the first time, it's good
to tie his halter rope to a log or a big rock or something that
he can drag just a little bit but can't run away with. This
lessens the danger of a horse injuring his neck at the withers
while pulling back and it keeps him from winding up with
a strained neck, commonly referred to as having his head
pulled down.

I roped three more big horses—two more bays and a blue
roan and we staked them out in about the same manner
that we did the first one. They had about twenty feet of
rope apiece that they could get tangled up in and rope-burn
their legs maybe during the night, all of which would make
them have a little more respect for that head rope when we
untied them the next morning.

During this horse scuffle, Old Friole couldn't keep his
eyes off of the fun, and like all top hands that have aged
out, he hollered lots of advice and funny conversation but
never did quit chunkin' up the fire around supper.

I guess this glade where we had camped on the side of
the road was about four or five acres and there was plenty
of room for the horses to scatter out and graze. When we
moved horses down a public road and camped at night, we
didn't worry too much about them driftin' in the direction we
were drivin' them because horses that have been driven far

enough will be tired and won't drift too far, and we would be able to pick them up the next morning when we broke camp.

All livestock, especially horses, are bad to try to turn back at night the way you brought them during the day, so after supper me and Choc backed up away from camp where the road was a little narrow. We both took a night horse and a little feed with us and tied our horse up kind of short on a stake rope. One of us got on each side of the public road, so that if any of 'em turned back in the night maybe we could booger 'em with a blanket afoot or, if we had to, we could saddle a night horse and take after 'em. The grass was good and fresh and there was water in the road ditch, so we didn't have any trouble that night.

While Friole fried some meat and made some biscuits for breakfast, me and Choc untied our wild horses. They all had been up and down during the night from being tangled up in the rope, and you could tell that this roan horse was going to be boogery and hard to ride because he had been nervous all night and had pulled his big rock about fifty feet and had managed to rope-burn every leg from a little to a whole lot.

As we untied these horses, Choc would help hold them. Anybody that knows anything about horses never walks up to a bronc and tries to rub him on the nose or between the eyes because that is a horse's blind spot and he can't see your hand and you will be nearly or directly in front of him where he could put a front foot in your shirt pocket or maybe drive your hat down tighter on your head. So as I worked up to each one's head, I stood a little to the side and worked my hand around to the outside of his jaw where I would be in view of his eye on that side, then I very gently scratched his jaw and under his chin until I could get my fingers in the corner of his mouth. I worked my fingers on the gum along and in front of his jaw teeth until he began to relax a little. As I tickled his gums and scratched the top of his mouth, he would open his mouth and lick his lips and work his tongue and while he was doing that I would be lookin' at his teeth to see how old he was.

Well, the three bays were four and five years old. The roan didn't think I smelt good and we backed him all over that glade trying to get up to his head. When I did manage to get my hand on the side of his jaw, he was snortin' a trombone tune that sounded like a declaration of war. He thought my hand tasted bad, but his nervousness caused him to work his mouth a lot quicker than any of the others had. Not much to my surprise but very much to my dislike, I found out that he was a smooth-mouthed horse and must have been about ten years old and had never done his part by packin' a man around in his lifetime, and whatever I was doin' or had in mind for him, he had already decided wasn't goin' to suit him.

As we broke camp and Friole drove his mule team out into the road behind the herd, we caught up with a few horses scattered up the road in front of us for maybe a couple of miles. These grass-fed soft horses were a little sore from the beginning of the drive and moved out in a walk and gave us no trouble to speak of during the day's drive. The horses draggin' halter ropes stepped on them a lot and pulled their heads a lot the first half a day. Then, as all horses will do, they went to walkin' holdin' their heads just a little sideways of the drag rope so that it would be to one side of where they were walkin'. This is just one of the ways horses will begin to smarten up when you start handling them.

We drove through Coleman that day and camped early in the afternoon at the edge of town by the side of the road where a little creek crossed. By now these horses were gettin' road-broke and stayed together good, and anytime we would let them stop, they would graze and rest and stay together. We caught the horses that we had haltered the night before and tied them hard and solid to mesquite trees. We thought we would leave them on a stout old tree during the night and let them find out that they couldn't break that batch of nuisance that they had on their heads.

Nobody had bantered us along the road to trade or buy horses, but some people had asked if we was takin' them to Brownwood. There was a horse and mule market at Brownwood that held an auction on Friday, which was two days and twenty-five miles away.

When I was restin' in the shade of the tree by the mercantile at Paint Rock waitin' for the ranch foreman to come in, I had dug down in my saddle bag and counted my money. I had had $1,004 besides a little change and I had spent $840 for the horses, which left me $164. By the time I paid for feed and camp at the wagonyard and bought the wagon and rigged it out to use, I was down to $80; then we bought a little stuff along the way for the next couple of days, which left me a little over $60. Friole and Choc wasn't worryin' about my money trouble and I hadn't discussed it with them, but I thought that if there was a horse and mule sale at Brownwood, I had better sell a few head before I went to runnin' low on travelin' money.

We drove into Brownwood the next day without too much happenin' along the way and drove our herd of horses past the Brownwood Horse and Mule Market and down to the railroad, where the stock pens were. I thought that we needed to be there all the next day and let our horses and mules fill up and maybe use the railroad stock pens to rope out and take what I wanted to sell up to the Brownwood Horse and Mule Barn the afternoon before the sale the next day.

While we were loafin' around the day before the sale and lettin' our horses graze along the road and along the railroad right of way, Friole took about half a day off and went into town and bought a few things that we needed in camp. Me and Choc saddled the horses that we had put a drag rope on and I snubbed them on old Beauty and Choc rode them.

They were pretty snuffy and tried to buck and did most of the layin' down and gettin' up that wild horses do when you are saddlin' them, but they didn't booger Beauty none and if they boogered me I didn't let Choc find out. He did a pretty fair job of sackin' and sweatin' out the first three. We ate a big dinner and laid around camp until middle of the afternoon and I brought up the little matter of that roan horse. Choc said, "Well, he's old enough now, and we'd better try him 'fore he puts some more age on."

I cinched old Beauty up pretty tight and rode in and picked up the halter rope and managed to draw him up to my saddle horn. I had three wraps on the saddle horn with the lead rope when he rared up to get away and found out that Beauty had different ideas about it. He decided if he couldn't go back'ards, he'd go for'ards, and when I saw his forefeet comin' where I was sittin, I swung out of the saddle and hung in one stirrup and held on to the snub rope and hid my head behind old Beauty's neck. Well, she wasn't goin' to put up with that, so she ducked out from under him real handy-like and I rolled back up in the saddle. Choc said, "I don't think he likes us, especially you."

And I said, "Well, no closer than you're gettin' to him, he couldn't have anything against you."

He was holding his saddle in one hand and a blanket in the other and this complimentary conversation from me braved him up some. As he started into that old roan, Roany hit the saddle with one foot and the blanket with the other and Choc fell about ten feet away with the blanket over his head like he was goin' to try to fake a dead instead of tryin' to ride that horse.

We didn't have any onlookers, so we didn't care too much about the show Roany was puttin' on. I didn't want his front feet and his open mouth in the saddle with me, so I worked Beauty closer to him until I had his head snubbed against the saddle. His mouth was open and slobber was runnin' from him and he may have had it on his mind to bite somebody or something. I stuck the halter rope under my left knee so I could squeeze it against the saddle and then threw my reins down on Beauty's neck and reached over with both hands and twisted both ears until I settled his nerves and he stood still for Choc to saddle him.

It was Choc's saddle and I asked him if he minded just turnin' him loose in the stock pen with it on. He said, "That saddle might save me some hide that way, so let's let him wear it awhile."

I slipped the halter rope off of my saddle horn, and when he found out he was loose, he bucked out high, wide, and handsome with that saddle and hit the ground so hard he popped the stirrups over the top of the saddle. Choc said, "I'm sure glad I didn't get on!"

In the late afternoon we picked out six of the fat, gentle, old ranch horses that we could do without; I knew the un-broken horses would get more ridin' with these gentle horses gone. I felt like we needed two teams of mules so we could take our time about working them to the camp wagon, but I didn't need three teams of mules, so we took the six old horses and a team of the oldest-lookin' but fat mules down to the auction barn and checked them in with the barn foreman for the Friday sale.

Friole had bought some fresh beefsteaks in town and some other out-of-the-ordinary kind of grub for a camp wagon and we had a big feast about dark and then all went to bed.

Next morning after breakfast, Friole said if we would leave a horse saddled, he would watch after the herd and keep them kind of bunched together while Choc and I went to the horse sale. At the auction barn, we saddled up our gentle horses one at a time and rode them up and down the alleys and got as many people to notice and ride and try them as we could.

There was a fast mule and horse buyer at the sale from Vicksburg, Mississippi, by the name of Ray Lum. He was always ready to buy gentle horses that didn't sell too high and would buy a mule of any description and as many of them as the market afforded. It was true that he might be a hard bidder and a mean buyer, but in the years to come I would know that Ray Lum, with all his faults, was a good man to have at an auction barn because he would put a starting bid on any kind of a horse or mule that came in the ring.

My fat gentle horses brought a total of $90 and Ray Lum bought the pair of old mules for $70. The commission was $2 a head, and after a few other little expenses I got out with $140. This built my pocket money past $200. I bought some woven-grass halters that could always be found at a horse and mule barn for 45¢ apiece and I thought we needed twenty of 'em, so that was another $9 spent—but these extra halters would make it easy for us to have a lot more horses draggin' rope as they drifted down the road.

We grazed our horses low and rode some of 'em part of the day as we began to get 'em gentle, and drifted into Bluffdale the next Tuesday night. A good many fellows that we met in cars or passin' along the road had begun to ask about the price of horses and wanted to look and walk through them, but we really hadn't had any cash buyers. There was some open land along the railroad track and over on the school ground where we camped at Bluffdale.

We had gotten far enough along on this drive that we had left the big ranch country behind us and were driving through a mixed ranch and stock farm country where there were no big bands of range horses and the price of horses had begun to change. I didn't really know how much the price had changed in the two hundred miles that we had covered, but I had learned at a tender age that when you priced a horse too high, you could always come down, but if you priced him too cheap, you were due to be cheated, so everytime I priced a horse I was kinda testin' the local market.

A fellow that was ridin' south rode by our camp leadin' a

pretty good farm chunk kind of work mare that was about eight years old and had harness marks on her that showed she would work. He said he would like to trade her for one of those young riding horses. He picked out one of the chestnut stocking-legged horses that we had by now ridden three or four times and asked how much for him. Well, I knew he wasn't fixin' to buy him and that this was goin' to be a trade deal, so I said, "Seventy-five dollars."

He said, "I guess I'd give about a third of it."

I said, "That would be about the right amount of difference between the mare you're leadin' and the horse you picked out."

He took a slobberin' fit about what a good mare he had and I gave him a pretty big talk about how little $25 was. After he had set around and ate up a batch of Friole's grub and drank half a pot of coffee and he could see I wasn't weakenin', he paid me the $25 out of his pocket. The chestnut horse was draggin' a lead rope and was no trouble to catch so we changed halters and he left the work mare and rode on.

Well, that helped my assortment of stock because I didn't have any work mares and when you go to mixin' them up, you've got different kinds of horses to appeal to different kinds of people and, besides, the money I got in the trade was a little more than three times what I paid for the chestnut horse, which was proof the horse market was going up as we traveled east.

About middle of the next morning we stopped at Tolar to rest our horses and hoped we might do some more business. Sure enough, in a little while there was a fellow wanted to trade four spotted Shetland pony mares. One was real old and she was the mama and grandmama of the rest of them and they were all man-broke and kid-spoilt. I hated to trade the working mare so quick but she was one he picked out. Then he wanted one of the work mules to go with her. I didn't much like this deal since this would leave me just one team of mules, so I got pretty hateful with him and he gave me $40 and the four Shetland ponies for the old mule and the work mare.

I don't think that I was as proud of these trades as Choc and Friole were because they really took on about how good we was doin'.

I had written my daddy a postcard from Comanche, Texas, tellin' him about what day we would reach Granbury, which was about twenty miles south of Weatherford, and sayin' that if he had time, he could come down to see my stock. We camped on the bank of the Brazos that night just east of Granbury and Daddy drove up a little before dark. We walked around and looked at my horses and he thought I must have found a sucker out in the West where I bought 'em.

Well, my daddy wasn't a horse trader and didn't pretend to be and never did give me any stagnatin' amount of advice, and after we had a little visit, I gave him $200 to put in the bank for me when he got home. I told him I had lots of horses to turn into money and I didn't know how long it would take, but I was going by the home place at Cumby in a few days and leave Charlie and Beauty in the pasture so I wouldn't have to ride 'em back from the end of the trip when I sold out—wherever that was goin' to be.

Early the next morning a cowboy that I knew by sight rode up to the camp wagon. I hadn't had any business with him, but he came to Weatherford to First Monday Trade's Day and that's where I had seen him. We visited a few minutes and I had already saddled a horse, so we rode around through the herd as they grazed.

When we stopped under the shade of a big pecan tree, he began to tell me that he was a little short of money or he would be glad to buy some horses. He went on to say that he was going to have a good deal of work to do horseback this summer and he wished he could buy two good young horses. He pointed out the ones he wanted on credit and said he would pay me that fall.

Well, I hadn't had much experience in the credit business, but I had lots of horses that hadn't cost much. While we were talking, a bright idea struck me and I said, "How about takin' those two horses and another one that I'll pick out and you break and have the use of the three of 'em and sometime in September you can have your pick of the three for breakin' the other two for me."

He liked this deal. It would give him plenty of horses to ride through the summer and wind up with one in the fall without being out any money. We roped out his horses and shook hands over the trade. Friole and Choc had camp-broke and we started the day's drive.

We camped on Mary's Creek the next night. By now, me and Choc had about fifteen head of young horses we could catch and saddle without having to snub 'em. Early the next morning before we left Mary's Creek, a Mr. Charlie Corn came by and said he had heard we was camped down there with a bunch of horses and he needed some young horses for his cowboys.

We walked around through the bunch and I pointed out the ones that had been rode a few saddles, and the ones that were unbroke, and I told him that those that had been rode were about $10 a head higher than the ones we hadn't done any work on. He said that would mean about $25 and $30 a head. I said, "I'm glad you ain't doin' my figurin'. That would be about $35 and $45 a head."

He said, "I've got cowboys that don't have enough to do. How about me buyin' six unbroke ones and pickin' 'em for $30 a head?"

I didn't think he could hurt the bunch much by pickin' 'em because they were all pretty much the same and you always stood a chance that he might accidently take a bad one. He wasn't tryin' to jaw me too much on my $35 price, so I sold him six head for $180. As he picked them, he came to the blue roan horse and said, "His head is skinned up. Did he ride good?"

I said, "To tell you the truth we caught him, but we didn't get around to ridin' him."

He said, "Well, I wouldn't want to pay any extra for him being caught, but I would take him in the bunch."

I had to frown at Choc to keep him from bustin' out laughin', but we made the deal. As he pointed out his horses, we worked 'em back to the end of the bunch and drove 'em about two miles and turned them into his ranch pasture gate.

We traveled slow that day and got way up high on a prairie west of Fort Worth where they were layin' out the streets for what was to later be Ridglea addition. The grass was good and there was more people passin' by and I thought we ought to graze the horses there a day or two and maybe sell some of 'em to the people that lived in the Town Where the West Begins.

This herd of horses on the west townsite of Fort Worth didn't create much commotion and we didn't have any lookers much less buyers. However, our horses filled up good on that blue-stem sage and were rested for the drive through Fort Worth. Early one morning we headed 'em right down Camp Bowie Boulevard and went across the Trinity River bottom.

As we topped out on the other side of the ridge, we were gettin' into a pretty prominent kind of residential district. We turned 'em down a street to the south until we hit a street running east and west parallel to the railroad track. We drove 'em on east on this street running north of the depot and at the south end of the business district and dropped off of the hill where the main town is and followed the main highway from Fort Worth through Arlington and Grand Prairie.

We were up on a high strip of country where there were very few houses and no business district and were grazin' our horses in the late afternoon close to the Trinity Portland Cement plant. There was some small pastures around this cement plant with great big fine fences and cement fenceposts. I saw a company car comin' out from the main plant with a sign on the side of it, so I loped up and waved and hollered until the man stopped.

He was a nice kind of fellow and got out of the car and looked up the road at my horses. I told him I was huntin' a place to pen 'em for the night and he pointed to a gate to one of these small pastures and told me it would be all right to turn them in there for the night if we were moving on the next morning. I told him that would sure be a fine place to camp with 'em inside those high fences and asked him what it would cost to pasture my stock and camp there for the night. He said, "Don't worry about it, son. When the man catches up with you that owns them, he can come over to the office and see about that."

The horses were a little leg weary from the day's drive and there had been a right smart of traffic. We had choused them off the pavement and along the bar ditches pretty steady all day and they hadn't had time to graze, so when I threw this big swingin' gate back, it was easy to point the herd into the pasture. There was a windmill and a water tank a short way from the gate where Friole pulled the wagon and started making camp for the night.

Next morning this nice man that had told me we could camp there drove down to the wagon early enough to have breakfast with us. He was a good fellow and I guess had some stock in his background because he seemed to enjoy walkin' through the herd of horses and pickin' out various ones to comment on. When he had had about his third cupful of coffee, I said, "That man that owns the horses would be glad to settle with you for the night's grazin'."

He said, "I thought he would be here this morning."

As I pointed to myself I said, "He's been here all the time."

By this time he knew my given name and he said, "Ben, a kid like you don't own this many horses."

It took some convincing on the parts of Choc and Friole

and they explained to him the distance we had come and that they were actually my horses and that we had started to East Texas to sell them. This fellow was a little past middle age and he sure began to get interested in this horse drive. He asked, "Do you all aim to go through Dallas with them?"

I told him I had been comin' from Cumby to Fort Worth all my life and I didn't know any way to get west of Dallas except to come through it or to get east of Dallas except to go through Dallas, and it must be the shortest way. I added the shortest way is the way you go with horses. He first laughed a little at that remark and then he said, "Ben, don't you think you're goin' to get into a whole lot of trouble taking these horses through Dallas?"

Me and Choc, being the wild rough young cowboys that we were, didn't know that there was anyplace that we couldn't drive a herd of horses, and I answered him by sayin', "Nope, I don't see how that herd of horses could cause me and Choc any trouble. We're ridin' good, shod, hard-fed, young horses that can outrun and outturn and outhandle any broncs or plainer kinds of horses and I don't see how they could give us any trouble that we can't handle. For a small bet, I think we could drive a few head of horses into the Jefferson Hotel and put 'em in the elevator for you."

With this batch of braggin' he kind of backed off and didn't say anything more about us havin' trouble with horses, but I could sure tell by lookin' at him that he didn't believe we could drive them half through Dallas without any trouble. I asked him again about payin' him and he said that this was the best breakfast he had since he moved to town twenty years ago and we didn't owe him nothin' for spending the night.

When he got in his car and drove off, he said, "I sure wish you luck on gettin' through town, but if I were you I would wait a little while till all these people going to work get out of the way."

I waved at him and hollered "Much obliged" as he drove off. Choc turned to me and said, "That feller thinks me and you are green hands at drivin' horses, don't he?"

I said, "I guess so, but this ain't a big enough bunch of horses to get away from me and you in just one town no bigger'n Dallas."

He kind of grinned at that and we went to saddlin' up and Friole had already broke camp and was harnessing up his mules. We hollered a few times and boogered these horses together and turned them into the road with Friole trottin' his mules to the camp wagon as he whistled some kind of Mexican tune.

We headed them east several miles on Davis Street. Sometimes we had as many cars mixed up in the herd as we had horses, but the cars that were meetin' us could pull over to one side and we would pass them. The cars that were goin' the same way we were were tryin' to work their way through the herd, but traffic wasn't really causin' us any particular trouble. When we came to Zangs Boulevard, we turned them north, and after we passed a park on the east side of the boulevard, this street made a curve and there was a down hill slope towards the Oak Cliff Viaduct. It's easy to get a herd of horses to move faster on a down slope, so we gave 'em a pretty fast push, intendin' to get them on the viaduct between the concrete banisters before they had time to think about it.

Now, the Oak Cliff Viaduct is about a mile long and was the first big viaduct crossing the Trinity River bottom ahookin' Oak Cliff and points west across to main Dallas and all points east. I don't know how far up in the air it is, but it's plenty high because lookin' down from the top of it at a railroad car below, the railroad car don't look much bigger than a Studebaker wagon.

There was a lot of cars meetin' us and goin' on by and there had begun to be a few cars behind us that had to slow up, but we were ridin' in a lope and the herd was movin' in a long, swift trot when we met a new T Model truck full of crates of somethin' with a wagon sheet tied to the front of the bed and afloppin' in the breeze at the back, and that floppin' and poppin' wagon sheet stopped the herd. As they pulled to turn back, me and Choc built a fence around them ahorseback.

We had lost Friole and the camp wagon, but I could see him back toward the end of the bridge with cars all around that ball of little snorty West Texas mules and there wasn't a chance for them to run away because there was no place for them to go.

We had the traffic stopped goin' both ways and these horses were millin' in the middle of the bridge and of all the honkin' and hollerin' and help we were gettin' from them people sittin' behind steerin' wheels, you never saw the like.

We were just about over the middle of the river channel, and after about ten minutes of this horse fright, there was motorcycle policemen comin' from every direction. One of 'em rode up kind of close to me and went to hollerin', askin' where the man was that owned these horses. Between fightin' horses and wavin' and hollerin', I told him he was talkin' to him. He said, "Kid, you don't own much more than the shirt on your back. Where's the man that owns these horses? Is he back there in that wagon?"

I said, "You can go see." I thought that would be a way to get one of these motorcycles out of the way.

He rode back and by now Old Friole was scared to death and couldn't speak a word of English, but he waved and made signs and pointed back to me. Another one of them motorcycle policemen was explainin' to me the traffic law and that I had the bridge blocked and I would have to move the horses. I was cowboy'n' all the time, hollerin' and squallin' and workin', and hollered back, "If you would move some cars, I could move some horses."

By now you could see cars stacked back to the west on Zangs Boulevard and you could see cars stacked back to the east past the depot. About that time, a train engine ran under the bridge somewhere and blowed the whistle. This bunch of West Texas ranch horses didn't know what that noise was, nor where it came from, but if they could have gone straight up, they would sure have got away from it.

The concrete banister on the viaduct was about three or four feet high and when that train whistle blew a second time, one of them wild, bald-faced, stocking-legged chestnut horses came out of the mill and cleared that railing. I stood in my stirrups and looked over the banister. She was fallin' through the air so fast that her mane and tail was stickin' straight up. I hollered at Choc, "I guess we had one too many, anyhow."

At quick glance I saw several more horses comin' across the bridge that was fixin' to follow suit and go over the rail. I spurred old Beauty right into 'em and squalled right loud, and when I did, I pushed three head onto the footbackers' sidewalk which was built along the concrete banister. When they started threadin' down that sidewalk that gave me an idea. As I started down the sidewalk, I hollered and pushed these three to keep them goin' and squalled at Choc to pour the rest of them in behind me.

A motorcycle policeman was meetin' them and I squalled at him to get out of the way. He didn't have time to turn that thing around so he pulled it out of the way while we pushed a hundred head of horses by him.

There was a park about a block big east of the depot and south of the Jefferson Hotel. I broke my horse into a run when I hit that grass and headed off the horses in front of me and threw them into a mill and held them there while Choc brought the rest of them down the sidewalk.

Range or gentle horses chum up in small bunches and graze and stay together and when one gets away from the others, they start nickerin' back and forth to locate one another. Now while these horses were in the excitement and milling in a bunch on the viaduct, they weren't making any extra noise, but when they got strung out single file for a half mile comin' down that footwalk off the viaduct, a lot of them got separated from one another and began to nicker in almost plaintive tones of excitement for their runnin' mates.

While all of this was goin' on, the bald-faced horse that went over the banister must have fallen in deep water because she had heard the nickerin' and had come up the side. As the rest of the herd came off of the bridge, she came out from under it and joined the herd. She was covered with a thin, nasty kind of water and mud and her mane and tail was soppin' wet.

I noticed a big water fountain sprayin' in the air but I didn't think these old ponies needed to stay there to drink, so I rode into them and broke the mill and turned them to drive off the park. Choc had worked around and was in front and he took the lead.

As we turned them off the park onto Houston Street, one of the motorcycle policemen was gonna hurry the drive and he rushed in close and raced his motor. When he did, the muddy-tailed horse swatted him across the face and knocked his cap off and plastered him with mud. His motorcycle threw him and ran wild into the horses before it fell over on its side. As I rode past it, I hollered back, "That's all right, Mr. Officer. I don't believe that thing hurt any of 'em."

When the leaders got to Pacific, I hollered and waved to Choc to point 'em east. People were tryin' to cross the street and cars were comin' and goin' and we had a few human stock mixed up in the drive once in a while but they managed not to get hurt. I didn't know exactly what was happening with the rest of the traffic at the stoplights because that bunch of ranch horses didn't seem to know the signals and they just kept goin' at a pretty high lope.

Somebody or something kind of broke the herd into where all that bunch of streets cross at St. Paul Street and some of the horses were about to turn south. I saw a man that was a friend of my daddy's that was in some kind of electric power business in Dallas named John W. Carpenter. I stood in my stirrups and squalled loud enough to shake the bricks on some of the tops of those buildings and hollered, "Mr. Carpenter, head them damn horses and don't let them go down that street!"

I glanced up and saw people's heads stickin' out of every window in them tall buildings awatchin' the last trail drive through downtown Dallas.

Old Man Carpenter grabbed his hat and squalled and hollered and turned them horses, and the way he was working at it, you would have thought they were his own. About the time I got even with him, three or four fellows was slappin' him on the back and braggin' on him, and I hollered, "Much obliged!" As I waved at him, I said, "You would've made a good hand if you'd stayed in the country."

I don't know whether traffic was gettin' normal behind us or not but it was gettin' thin and wasn't causin' the horses too much trouble in front of us. I squalled at Choc and he began to holler and fight them back with his hat to slow up the drive. I dropped back enough to give them a little air without gettin' to where I couldn't move in if I needed to.

As we drove up Gaston Avenue where there were big fine homes on both sides, these horses were wringin' wet with sweat and latherin' and blowin' and they slowed down to a walk and none of 'em tried to cross the sidewalk and get up into anyone's yard. By now 'most everybody we met in cars were stoppin' and lettin' us drive past them. We were hazin' the horses a little to one side of the street and there were a few cars working through them. Now and then you would hear a fender bump and there might have been a headlight or two got kicked out during the drive. However, I didn't try to find out about little details like that.

As Beauty hit a nice slow foxtrot following the herd, I took off my hat and wiped the sweat from my head. I began to think a little about what that man over at the cement plant meant when he said we might have some trouble. We had long since lost Friole, and I knew he had gone crazy with fright but I didn't know whether he had turned back to go to Mexico or was still followin' us.

We came to a nice big open spot to the south side of the street and some of the horses drifted over on it a little bit, and here come a bunch of grown men wearin' kids' knickerbocker britches and caps and wavin' clubs in the air. I guess that was the first time I realized that golf players were one of the more excitable breeds of people, so while Choc rode point, I winged them on the side and got them off without causin' too many new holes in that pasture pool ground.

Along about middle of the afternoon, we watered our horses at the spillway of White Rock Dam. Since we was kind of in the country, we held them up and let them shade and rest a little while. There was a hamburger joint across and back from the road a little piece, and it took a batch of 'em to fill up me and Choc after that morning's drive. When all the horses looked like they had cooled out pretty good, we eased them out up the road in a walk and let them graze.

A little before sundown, we drove onto the square at Garland. I knew there was a big red mule barn with some pens around it across the railroad track on the east side of the business part of town, and we headed them for that barn. In the summertime the work mule and horse business slacked up and Mr. Pace, who owned the barn, wasn't anywhere around, so I opened the gates and stocked his mule barn with West Texas ranch horses and shut the gate and looked back and thought about how much trouble we might have had if we hadn't been real good cowboys.

This herd of horses had endured a pretty bad beatin' from civilization and its ills, such as traffic, hard-paved streets, and gravel-surfaced roads, and they all showed the effects of the day's drive. I had been on my best horse, Beauty, all day and Choc had been riding my other favorite mount at the time, Charlie. These horses had whirled and turned and jumped and stopped a few hundred times apiece that day and you could say they were badly spent, but Friole and the camp wagon were still lost. I told Choc to unsaddle and stay with the horses and I would ride Beauty back and look for Friole.

Beauty was at this time an eight-year-old and had been my favorite mount for several years. She was fourteen hands three inches tall and had a huge rib cage and heart-lung capacity, and even though she was not a tall horse her body girthed down way below the bottom of my stirrups. Her legs were straight and sound, her back short, and it was un-believeable how much endurance she had as compared to other horses. Going back to look for Friole could have run into an all night's job, but on Beauty I would still not have been afoot.

I rode onto Friole about two miles outside of Garland. His mules were wet with sweat and had been latherin' under the harness most of the day. He was sure glad to see me and hoped it wasn't too much farther to the herd. He said that them cars had all time been in the way and that his team had all time been scared but they couldn't run away 'cause there was too many people in front of them. I asked him how he knew which way to come after we were out of sight. He said, "The sign from a hundred head of horses wasn't so hard to follow."

When Friole and I got to Mr. Pace's barn, we drove the wagon into the hall of the barn and unhitched the team. About that time, Mr. Pace heard about the horses and drove up in front. I walked out and shook hands and told him that I knew him from seein' him at the Fort Worth Horse and Mule Market and thought that it would be all right to use his barn even though I hadn't asked him about it. He said, "Why sure, you're welcome, and I'll be down here early in the morning to sell a bunch of these horses for you before you leave town."

I asked him about buying some hay and he told me that

all last year's crop of hay had been fed up but there was about half a crib of corn in the barn. The weevils would eat it up before he would need it this fall and he thought it would be just the right thing to throw out in the troughs for my horses, shuck and all. That sounded good to me and tasted good to them.

By now it was night and the three of us went over to the best restaurant in town and ordered enough for us and several more people. Then the three of us ate all of it.

I unfurled my bedroll in the hall of the barn under the wagon and Choc slept in front of the corral gate on the outside just in case something might happen in the night and Old Friole always slept in the wagon. About the nicest sound that can put a cowboy to sleep at night is to hear a good horse that's rode hard all day grinding oats or corn. All the horses were tired and there was no fightin' going on and that ear corn made sweet music as I dozed off.

The next morning our horses were still drawn and showed lots of signs in their feet and legs from the drive on hard city streets the day before. Mr. Pace came to the barn pretty early and said he thought it would be good for the horses if we would stay a few days and feed them the rest of that corn, and this would also give him a chance to sell a few horses for me.

While we were talking, we walked around and he asked me questions about the different horses and how much money I would have to have for each individual that we looked at. I knew that he would expect to make some money on the deal for himself, so I added a little to the price to use for tradin' purposes and a little more to pay him for his time and efforts. He seemed to think I had most of the horses priced a little cheap, and when we came to the four Shetland ponies he said, "I've got people that've been cryin' for Shetlands to ride this summer. Hope you haven't bought these so high that they will be hard to sell."

I said, "How high would that be, Mr. Pace?"

He said, "I believe they will bring $75 to $100 a head if you can stand to take that for 'em."

I was laughin' inside and tryin' to keep it from showin' when I told him that I would try to stand it and for him to go ahead and sell 'em.

He and I agreed that these horses were drawn pretty bad from the Dallas trail drive and that it would be better for them to rest and fill up before we started showing them to his prospective buyers the next day.

The next morning he circled around town a little while and me and Choc caught the horses he had asked about the day before that he thought would suit his customers. We brushed and curried their manes and tails and cleaned them up as best we could and put nice halters on them and tied them up and down the hallway of the barn.

Pretty soon after dinner, Mr. Pace had a lot of lookers come that were interested in some kind of a horse. Me and Choc were busy during the afternoon saddlin' horses while Mr. Pace rared back on his walkin' cane, and with the aid of some strong spirits, he made some vigorous sales talks. I don't really know whether it was his salesmanship or that the people just wanted the horses, but we did a big day's business. By night he had sold all the Shetlands and four other young horses for cash and we hadn't taken anything in for trade.

I asked Mr. Pace that night what I owed him. He said, "You never have said what the horses cost, so I don't know how much money you're makin' and I'll leave it up to you to pay me what you can stand."

Well, he hadn't been very timid pricin' those horses that day and everything had sold for as much or more than I had told him to get for them. I had done him the favor of eatin' up that corn that the weevils might get and used his barn, so I asked if I could square off with him for his services and the use of his barn for a hundred-dollar bill.

Hundred-dollar bills were scarce and Mr. Pace had been paid a hundred-dollar bill for one of the Shetlands. He laughed and said that smaller money would spend better, but that he would be well pleased with the amount, so we had a laugh and I paid him in smaller money and stuffed that hundred-dollar bill in the bottom of my saddlebag.

The next morning we pushed the gates open and Mr. Pace said, "Go ahead. I'll shut the gates when you're gone."

Our horses had been in the corral on dry corn for two days and they were all ready to graze some green grass along the road and were givin' us no trouble drivin' down the highway. Friole's team was comin' along by themselves because Friole was takin' a siesta. This city horse drivin' had been keepin' him from gettin' his rest.

We let the horses drift as slow as they would and graze as much as they would and we weren't tryin' to make any particular place before dark. In the late afternoon we were in a river bottom and ahead of us high up on the hill was the town of Rockwall, the county seat of Rockwall County, the smallest county in the state.

All the land along the road was in farms and I had begun to watch for a fenced pasture where we might camp our horses overnight. The land along the highway and the rich black land delta wasn't even fenced on the road and farmers drove out to the end of the row and turned on the bank of the bar ditch so I knew that we were going to have trouble finding a camp ground to hold herd on that night. I told Choc to graze 'em on into town and I would ride on ahead and see if I could find a place for us that night.

Beauty hit a good, swinging foxtrot and I got away from the herd fast and rode in on the square and hitched her to a telephone pole. I walked over to a drugstore and went to inquirin' around for a place for my horses. The druggist and some other natives first thought that I was tryin' to find a place for me and my horse and suggested I could put my horse in the gin lot or somebody's backyard. It was a little hard for a kid to convince these natives in a farm country that there was ninety-seven head of horses just over the ridge and comin' into this farming town. None of them knew anybody that had a town lot big enough to keep them overnight.

The more I inquired the less I found out, and a bowl of chili and two Cokes later, the horses began to top the ridge and the leads started trottin' on to the square. I got on Beauty and whistled and called to the herd and they started followin' me off the other side of the square. I hollered back at Choc when he came in sight that we might spend the night on the road. He knew what I said. He also knew what I meant— that we would find a camp somewhere. The highway wound out of town through the residences and made a curve to turn back east at a little creek just out of sight of the houses. Where the road turned, there was a big gate with high posts and an arch overhead that said ROCKWALL CITY PARK. Now this country town park didn't amount to much more than a see-saw, a swing, and a sandbox on the bank side of the creek near the gate.

It was nearly sundown and I could tell that there was a lot of tall grass on the back side of the park that looked to me like it had about twenty or twenty-five acres in it. I suddenly knew that this band of horses was bound to enjoy the good park facilities of Rockwall, so I dropped back down the highway below the gate and pointed them into the fresh creek water and tall grass. Friole was bringing up the tail of the herd with the camp wagon and he gave off a big smile. As he waved his sombrero at the trees and runnin' water he said, "*Muy buena, enoche.*"

Friole drove the wagon to the back side of the park and made camp under some big trees by the creek. Me and Choc pushed the horses up on a high place in the back side of the park where the grass was good. By this time the herd drove good and would graze good from the standpoint that they would always be tired enough to graze and rest and wouldn't hunt ways to get away.

There wasn't any buyers or horse traders followed us into camp that night and we were back away from the road. After several days of people and highways and short night quarters, this was a real nice camp.

Friole had breakfast ready way before daylight. It had become our custom to carry a sack of oats in the back of the camp wagon that we always fed our saddle horses, so Choc and I fed the horses and let them eat while we ate.

We caught the mule team and harnessed and hooked them up while Friole broke camp and got ready to travel. By sunup we were a few miles away from Rockwall headin' on east toward Greenville when the high sheriff of Rockwall County drove past the herd, stopped, and got out of his car. I was ridin' wing on that side when he stopped me and asked, "Kid, where's the man that owns these horses?"

I said, "I own 'em."

He looked at me pretty hard and said, "Kid, I'm talkin' business. I'm Earl Hall, the sheriff of Rockwall County, and I want to see the man that owns these horses."

Well, I kind of would liked to have changed the story by that time, but I said, "Can't help whether you believe me or not. I own the horses."

As the herd passed by us, you could see him sizin' up the horses and lookin' at Choc. As the wagon came up, he held his hand up for Friole to stop. He asked Friole if he owned the horses and Friole could see that big star on his chest, which scared off his United States vocabulary and in his fright he couldn't speak a word of English. The sheriff gave up on him and turned to me and said, "You owe a $25 fine for keepin' the horses in the Rockwall City Park last night."

He could have said, "You owe a $25 pasture fee," and I might not have thought anything about it, but that word fine had a bad sound to me. He was talkin' on and told me that if I couldn't pay it, he would put us all in jail. I said, "Well, I don't doubt but what the high sheriff of the smallest county in the state could put me and my cowboy and camp cook in jail, and if you've already decided about doin' that, I guess we can just turn these horses back in the park and go to jail."

He scratched his head and thought about that a few minutes and said, "Looks like you'd rather pay a fine."

I said, "Looks like you would have a better place to put my horses if I'm goin' to jail."

He kind of stomped the ground and said, "There aren't many people know about you stayin' in the park. Just don't come back." He turned around and went to his car and drove off.

From Rockwall on, the farther east we moved these horses, the more commotion they caused and the bigger the herd got in the minds of the people that saw them. A hundred horses wouldn't amount to much in the West but a hundred in this farming country was a sight to see and people would run out to the road from their houses to count and watch them pass. During the day, several farmers would stop and ask if we had a certain kind of horse.

We were grazin' the horses along the railroad track and highway as we drifted through Caddo Mills and a schoolteacher came up to the camp wagon and said he wanted to trade a fine-spirited horse that was too much for him to ride for something gentler. Choc and I had ridden all the ranch horses that we had kept and there were three of them that could stand a lot of ridin' and weren't too old. The rest of these horses could stand about half a day's ride before they gave out, even though they were in good flesh and looked like good stout horses.

Well, the schoolteacher picked out a brown horse and asked if we would saddle him up and ride him to show he was gentle. Choc caught and saddled him, and, of course, he rode gentle and stood still for you to get on and had a lot of good qualities to recommend him as a schoolteacher's horse, including a few mossy grey hairs under his foretop and around his ears.

I rode over to his horse as he walked along by my horse to look at what he had to trade. His horse was a light dun in color and would be big and tall for a cowboy to mount and a heap taller than that for a schoolteacher to get on. He said that he was mean to rare up and that he had rather not try to ride him to show him to me.

This horse had a good six-year-old mouth and it looked like everything else was good about him but his disposition, so after a good deal of conversation I squeezed that schoolteacher from $15 boot and led the dun horse back to the wagon. The schoolteacher got the old brown horse and jumped on him bareback and rode home happy.

I turned the big horse loose with the rest of the herd and we began to push them toward Greenville. This herd of horses comin' down Lee Street, which is the main street of town, caused a lot of farmers and town people to stop and look and run out the front doors of their businesses to see the sight. Of course, I knew lots of people since I had ridden away from here just four years before, and I had a lot of wavin' and hollerin' and braggin' to do as we drove 'em on down and put 'em in the trade pens at the old Ingram Wagonyard.

The black-land natives gathered around these horses the next morning and we had some tradin' business. We traded the odd mule that we had besides our team for a good-lookin' high-headed saddle horse. I had a weakness for these high-headed saddle horses and I gave $25 boot. Old Friole said he was afraid the heat was affectin' me because all this time he had never seen me pay anybody else boot in a horse trade. Choc thought this was funny and Friole got a big kick out of hurrahin' me about "givin' away" money.

I traded a pair of matched five-year-old stocking-legged, bald-faced chestnut horses to Al Eiland, who was an old-time friend of mine and a very fine horseman. He traded me a nice fox-trottin' saddle mare even for the pair. She was "open in the corners," which meant she was an eight-year-old, and

I felt like I had graduated to a top horse trader anytime I could cheat Mr. Eiland, and I knew for sure that I had cheated him.

The next day we turned out of the wagonyard and drove out on Johnson Street and out by the fairgrounds to where we hit the Lone Oak Road. Then I left Choc and Friole to drive the herd of horses on to Emory, which was about twenty-five miles and told them to trade for whatever they saw that they thought they would like.

I took Beauty and Charlie and led a good grey horse and went to Cumby, fifteen miles, where I left Beauty and Charlie in the old home pasture where Beauty was born. I spent the night at the old home place and next morning I left early and rode south through Miller Grove.

Late that afternoon, I found the herd of horses grazin' along the creek south of Emory. Friole had made horse trade. There was a farmhouse where a woman had some beautiful loud-colored bedspreads hanging on the line for sale. The one that Friole picked out had flowers and birds all colors of the rainbow woven into a bright red background. Friole picked it up off the wagon sheet and waved it in the air at me, laughin' and hollerin' *"Muy bonita manta,"* which meant "Very beautiful blanket." He had traded the oldest one of the gentle saddle horses for the beautiful blanket, two dozen eggs, and a gallon of sweet milk and was tickled with his trade, and I couldn't see how he hurt me much in the deal either.

Tied to the off front wheel of the wagon was a fat slick-haired young brush goat. When I noticed it, Friole began to laugh and Choc was tryin' to think of something else to do or somewhere else to go and I asked, "Friole, is that yours too?"

He said, "No, Señor Choc may settle down somewhere and wants a goat."

By this time Choc was kickin' his toe down in the ground and lookin' past my shoulder to explain the goat. He had asked a farmer $25 for another one of the old saddle horses that was gentle and the farmer offered him $15. Choc thought that was enough for the horse but he wanted to show his tradin' rights, so he told him he would take the $15 and that goat. Evidently there hadn't been much argument because there was the goat tied to the wagon wheel.

The next morning Choc said that he would like to ride the big dun horse that we got from the schoolteacher. I said, "We'll name him Professor. Get on and we'll see if he's got some smart."

I had saddled this good grey horse I had ridden to Cumby and Friole had broke camp and loaded the wagon with the iron skillets and red blanket and the pet goat and we were about ready to move herd.

Choc caught the dun horse without much trouble and as he saddled him, the horse showed to be shy and didn't want to stand to be saddled. Choc was havin' a good deal of trouble tryin' to get on him when I rode over and dropped a rope around the Professor's neck and snubbed him to my saddle horn. Choc was a good, stout, long-legged cowboy and got a hold and stepped on him in a hurry.

The Professor tried to make several wild lunges and the grey horse hadn't had enough schoolin' and we let him get about four feet of slack in the rope. He was rarin' up and looked like was goin' to fall back when I spurred my horse and brought him back to earth in a pretty forceful manner. I looked at Choc and he showed a little surprise and I said, "What do you think?"

He said, "I think in about three days from now he'll be a pretty gentle horse," and I reached over and untied the rope and turned him loose.

The herd wasn't much trouble to drive during the day and Choc and the dun Professor had one fight after another from balkin' to buckin' to runnin' away. He was sure spoilt and didn't intend to get over it fast.

We camped at Quitman the next night in an open glade

on the bank of a creek near town. As long as we were in the black land, farmers thought of these light-boned West Texas horses only as saddle horses because they were not big enough to be used for power in the heavy black soil. However, we were gettin' into deep East Texas, sandy-land country, where there was a better demand for smaller horses and the natives along the way were lookin' at these West Texas horses as work horses as well as saddle horses and business was pickin' up. We had a lot of visitors and talkers the afternoon that we camped but no sure 'nuff trades.

That night at camp I told Friole to stack everything out of the camp wagon on the ground next morning and take the wagon sheet and bows off because we were starting to use the camp wagon for a hitch wagon and sell some work horses.

I knew that we might have a few runaways and I wanted the wagon empty and our camp stacked all in one place. After breakfast we began to catch some of the horses that we had rode a few times because they would be sort of bridle-wise and we could hold them back or pull their heads around hooked to the wagon better than we could a raw bronc.

We hitched the gentlest and what we thought to be the stoutest mule on the right-hand side and after the battle of gettin' the harness on a pretty good size bay horse, we worked and pushed him around and got him up by the mule and tied a lead rope from his bridle reins back to the mule's hame. While I held him, Choc finished hookin' the traces and the breast choke and picked up the lines and got in the wagon.

This range-bred horse wasn't wearin' that mule harness with a whole lot of pride and you could tell by the way he had his ear cocked and the music rollin' out of his nose that he really wasn't plannin' on doing the right thing. I told Choc to stand real still and not breathe hard until I got on my grey horse that I was callin' Concho. I figured if we had a big runaway, I could ride into that unbroke horse and help change his mind.

I rode up by the side of the wagon and Choc spoke to the work mule and he moved off pullin' the wagon and the horse. When the horse set back and the wagon rolled up and hit him on the hocks and hindquarters he pulled that forward-lungin' act that you plan on when you are breakin' young horses to work to a wagon. This old mule was pretty wise and with the horse's head tied back to his hame, he just pulled to one side of the road and kept the wagon straight.

This bronc didn't throw no kickin' fits and we drove him out a country road about a mile and found a wide place to circle and turn around. By the time we got back to the camp, he was travelin' in a walk and tryin' to get along with all that harness afloppin' and poppin' around on him.

When a herd of horses is driven a few hundred miles, their feet wear off and break off and get just a little tender, and a tender-footed horse doesn't have to make but a few hard jumps and landings on a gravel- or hard-surfaced road until he begins to take a little more sensible view of tryin' to get along with his plight. This is one reason that I knew that it would only take two or three hitches on each one of these horses that we would offer to sell "gentle to work."

We put in the morning harnessin' and unharnessin' broncs and workin' them a little piece to the wagon. They actually put on a worse show and a bigger fit harnessin' than they did workin'.

The word had got around that there was some fresh horse stock in the country and the native farmers ridin' in a wagon or ridin' a work horse bareback and wearin' them bib over-alls had started gatherin' around the camp drinkin' coffee and atalkin' horses. Money must not have been too plentiful with them because they did a lot of feelin' and talkin' and lookin' on a horse before they got around to tryin' to buy him, but this was all right as long as there was more than one looking. As many horses as I had, I didn't have to spend much time with any one of them and when they finally made up their minds, we started talkin' trade.

When we worked these horses, we would drive them enough to break them into a sweat. Then we wouldn't clean them off when we unharnessed them because we wanted the harness marks to show that they had been worked. We sold five horses that day for cash and rehooked each one to show that they would work.

What our hookin' actually amounted to—it showed that you could harness and hook them to a wagon with a gentle mule. Actually, it was a poor test because we weren't recommending that they would pull to a load or had been worked in the field, but, anyway, when these overall-clad natives wearin' tennis shoes would see harness marks on one where the sweat had dried that was all it would take to get him interested.

The next day I traded two mares for two pairs of old mules that were small and fat with long manes and bushy tails that needed roachin' and cleanin' up, and in each trade I drew about as much money as I had paid for the horses, counting the expenses I had in 'em on the trip. When you are trading horses and you can draw about as much boot in a trade as your horse cost, you just do the farmer a favor by takin' whatever else he wants to give you in the way of horse stock so he can feel like he cheated you bad because he got rid of something that he didn't want.

I decided that we had had about all the quick horse business that we were going to have at Quitman, so Friole rerigged the camp wagon and early next morning we drove off from Lake Fork Creek where we were camped and started for Mineola. I thought this would be a good time for me to ride the nice fox-trottin' bay saddle mare that I had gotten from my friend Al Eiland in Greenville.

Our horses drove good and the mules that we had traded for didn't offer to turn back and this saddle mare was moving me around over the road in rockin'-chair fashion until we got to a little sandy-bottom creek that ran across the road and she stepped out into the water on her side and wallered like a dog, and me scufflin' to get off of her. I didn't seem to unnerve her a bit. Water ran into my boots and wet my little dry feet, and as it made me mad enough, I kicked her in the nose and belly and she seemed to be thoroughly enjoyin' herself and payin' me very little mind.

Choc looked back and saw the commotion and rode up on the bank on the Professor that he had straightened out into a pretty good horse. He thought that we were a pretty sight and he set there laughin' at me, which didn't help the situation any.

As the mare flounced a little bit with her head, I stumbled and fell over on her neck, which gave me a bright idea and I went up on her head and down in the water with it. I got one ear in my mouth and bit down on it hard and held her nostrils in that water until she went to blubberin'. As we started to come up, I turned loose of her ear and stepped back in the saddle as she rose out of the shallow water.

At noon we made camp long enough to cook and eat dinner by the side of the road and I tied this beautiful fox-trottin' water-dog mare to a tree with the bridle reins. I didn't much more than step away from her when she rared back, groaned, and broke the bridle reins. I hollered at Choc and he rode in and caught her by the head stall before she started back to Greenville.

I intended to tie her around her neck with a big hard rope that would sure enough hold her and then I decided I might not know all her bad habits yet. I didn't want her to skin her head and neck up from her settin' back atryin' to break a tree down because those kind of flesh scars don't improve the sales value of a horse, so I took a soft rope and wrapped it around 'her forelegs just above the angles and hobbled her and this sure was a shock to her sensitive high-tone nature. She wasn't tied but she couldn't leave and she spent the noontime workin' herself into a lather over those hobbles.

I normally would have changed horses at dinner but I felt like me and that little darlin' ought to get better acquainted, and I decided to ride her the rest of the day. Along about three o'clock in the afternoon because she was a soft, fat, town mare, she had gotten awfully tired and had begun to fight the bits and pull at the reins to go. I got a pretty firm hold on her and for some reason and she grabbed the bits between her teeth and cold-jawed and ran away with me.

I didn't know whether I could stop her or whether she would run into something, so I kicked both feet out of the stirrups and put one hand on the swell of the saddle and instead of pullin' on her I gave her slack. When she found out she wasn't in a fight and she was just making herself tired, she slowed up and stopped still. I let her stand there and shake and quiver and be mad until the herd caught up with us. I knew then that I had a town-spoilt mare and my friend Al Eiland had a nice pair of matched stocking-legged chestnut horses that were probably makin' a beautiful driving team, and I was the one that got cheated.

We camped in a grove of trees by the side of the road in the edge of Mineola that night and didn't do anything smart with our horses. Friole had begun to get used to some of the luxuries of farming country and had learned to stop along the way at farmhouses and buy fresh eggs and milk and the better kind of grub that was luxurious to a native from south of the border. I smelled something good cookin' for breakfast while I was feedin' my high-headed saddle horse that I was going to ride that day, and when I walked up to the campfire, Friole was all smiles. The day before he had bargained for some Dominicker chickens and we were havin' fried chicken for breakfast. It seemed to me that horse traders was livin' better than anybody.

Friole was a good cook even though his grub sometimes was pretty rank for bland-mouthed people—I'm sure that if he had made a pie, he would have had to put a little pepper and a pod of garlic in it.

I saddled my high-headed saddle horse that I had traded for at Greenville and just wondered if he was goin' to be any kin to the saddle mare. I thought I would go to town and loaf around a little bit and get a haircut and put out the word about havin' a herd of horses to sell and trade.

This nice high-headed horse was the right one to ride to town because when I

passed down the street everyone stopped to look at him. He carried you without any loss of motion, and the arch in his neck and the bow in his tail showed that he was real proud of himself. The town barbershop wasn't too excitin' and I didn't run into any real good horse conversation there or at the drugstore, and I decided I would ride around through the back of town where there ought to be some horse and mule barns and then go back to camp.

I was ridin' down the back street south of the business district and lookin' off awatchin' that horse's image travel in the plate glass windows he passed, which was a cowboy's way of showin' off. While I was settin' up straight and watchin' this nice horse in the windows, he rode right into a wagon that had its hind wheels stickin' out in the street, stumbled, and fell to his knees. While I was scufflin' to get his head back up, he was headed square dab into a wide post at the railroad crossing. I spoke to him and reined him up and got him stopped and I could tell that he was ashamed of himself and knew that he had done something wrong and was quiverin' all over but not offerin' to fight. There was an old man smokin' a pipe and strokin' his beard watchin' me and as I moved the horse off and passed by him, he said, "That's sure a nice horse to be moon-blind."

I let on like I didn't hear him but that word "moon blind" reverberated through my mind in a weird ghostlike voice. I didn't tell Choc nor Friole, and as I unsaddled him I brushed the dirt and loose hair off his knees the best I could with my bare hand.

That afternoon a dressed-up man and a little sissy fancy-dressed boy about fifteen years old drove up to camp in some kind of a long automobile and got out and started a conversation about wanting a saddle horse for the summer. As we talked on, the man went to telling the boy that they just might buy two horses and he might ride with him some and show him the finer points of horsemanship. This fellow seemed to be some kind of a railroad executive and early in his conversation went to telling me about being raised on fine horses back in Tennessee and for me not to bother with him until he had walked around through them and picked out what he wanted. He said, "I know horse traders always pick out what they want to sell, but I had rather pick out what I want to buy."

I told him that was all right. Just help himself.

Well, I guess he had had some fine horses in his bringin' up because he picked out the beautiful bay mare and the high-headed saddle horse for the two he wanted—he didn't know it but they were the two I wanted him to have bad. He asked if he could ride these horses, so Choc saddled up the mare and this fancy fellow rode her maybe half a mile down the road. There wasn't any creeks and he got off of her at the wagon. We didn't tie her and he asked, "How much for her?"

I said, "One hundred twenty-five dollars," knowing that was way too high, but I didn't know whether he knew it or not and I was really just testin' him.

He didn't answer back, but he said, "Let's see you ride the nice high-headed gelding."

Choc rode him and he started back toward the wagon and I stepped out and motioned to Choc to ride out toward the road. Well, this fancy man wanted to ride him, so he rode him down the straight road and back and got off him in the open. I breathed a horse trader's sigh of relief that he had got 'em both rode without them givin' away their secrets. You see, I suppose they were secrets because nobody had told me about their habits and ailments and I didn't feel like it would be appropriate for me to tell them either.

While I was breathing this sigh of relief, I heard him tell Choc that I looked a little young to be out selling horses. Well, Choc was a few years older and he told him that the horses were mine and that I could trade with him.

The fancy man said to me, "You wouldn't ask as much for him as you would the mare."

I said, "Yes, I would."

"I think they are too high and $100 apiece ought to be enough if I bought them both."

"Well, I might not feel that way about it, but since you are buyin' them and that's all you'll give, I'm gonna do without 'em for that little amount of money."

We gave him a couple of lead ropes and the little sissy boy was going to lead them to whereever they lived in town and the man was going to drive along in the long car and tell him how to do it.

Just as quick as they were out of hearing distance, I told Friole to catch his mules and break camp and get ready to move. I waved at Choc to come into camp and told him to bunch the horses up and start movin'. Well, he and Friole put up an argument about what a good campsite it was—it was late in the afternoon and we hadn't sold but two horses and we might be going off leavin' a lot of business. I said, "Yeah, but I don't want to be camping this close to town when the fancy man and that baby-faced boy try to get back home after their ride in the cool of the afternoon. They might cross a creek or the moon might come up wrong, and I think the grazin' would be better for this herd and we would probably get a better night's sleep seven or eight miles down the road."

We drove farther than that and made camp close to the town of Crow, where Lake Fork Creek runs into the Sabine River.

Next day we drove our horses on into Big Sandy and stopped out in the edge of town on a little creek and made camp early in the afternoon. I rode into town to buy some grub and see if I could find a feed store that would sell me a few sacks of oats. The feed store man had two big used saddles that were in real good shape and he wanted to trade 'em for a horse that was gentle to ride. This sounded like a good deal to me 'cause we could always use an extra saddle or two. It's good for a bronc horse when you're drivin' him down the road to wear a saddle and it might make it easier for somebody to get on him if he had it on for a day or two.

I went on back to camp and a little before dark, Mr. Feed Man drove up to camp with the oats that I had bought and his two saddles. He was driving a pair of nice, small, matched brown mares and you could tell at a glance from the frost around their ears and eyes that they had some age on them. Choc went to talkin' to him about tradin' him a pair of nice young horses for those mares.

Choc's horse tradin' argument by now had begun to get pretty good so the old feed man looked through our bunch and picked out a pair of young horses the same color as his mares and a little bigger than the mares. He asked a lot of questions and Choc had kind of took over the trade.

I was takin' a closer look at the mares when I heard Choc tell him that he would hook these horses and guarantee them to work and the reason he knew they was gentle was that he "drove" them right straight through downtown Dallas. That sounded like a good guarantee to the old man, so we got the horses and unhooked the mares and used the mares' harness and the old man's hack and he and Choc drove up and down the road four or five miles. This was a pair of young horses that we had put a good deal of breaking on and they didn't make a bad showing.

Friole had a good supper cooked in a little bit and the old feed man ate supper with us and traded us the two saddles for the difference in the mares and the young horses and drove his new team back to town after dark. I never knew whether or not the old man scattered any feed with his new team before he got them town broke.

We moved on through Longview the next day and didn't see any good camping places. It was really early in the day, so we moved on and made camp that night at Hallsville. Some farmers drove by in their wagons and stopped for a little conversation, but we didn't have any tradin' business and it was gettin' toward the end of the week.

We drove into Marshall the next day and were loose-grazin' our horses in the edge of town along the railroad track and highway. We had found a good place to camp by the side of the road where there was some big trees. Marshall was a big country town and everybody gathered in on Saturday. News travels fast by the grapevine and it seemed like everybody knew there was a bunch of tradin' horses down by the railroad stock pens. We had several lookers Saturday afternoon and made some fairly decent kind of horse sales without taking in any tradin' stock.

I rode uptown—I guess to do a little loafin'—and when I came back, Choc had been asleep under a big tree and Friole had disappeared. He showed up about time to fix supper and told us that he had found some *amigos* that worked for the railroad. There were six Mexican families camped on a switch track in house cars. This was a construction or repair crew that the railroad moved around to work on the track. They were all young men with families and some of them had been raised in South Texas on ranches and were better-than-average cowboys. Friole had had a big afternoon visitin' with them and they told him that since tomorrow was Sunday they would be over to look at the horses.

During the time Friole was fixin' supper, he said he sure thought it would be a fine time to butcher that fat goat we had been carrying with us and have a big barbecue for all his new friends. Well, I could understand Friole being a little lonesome for some of his own tribe and these were probably the first real South Texas Mexicans he had seen since we had left Ballinger. I knew that if these were young South Texas ranch-raised men that I might have a chance to get some cowboy'n' done Sunday on my bronc horses. One reason we hadn't butchered the goat was that three of us couldn't eat up a fresh goat and I thought that would be good bait to use to get some horse workin' done, so I told Friole to leave his supper pots and pans and go back to the railroad house cars and ask the men if they would like to have a big barbecue and ride horses Sunday.

It was probably a quarter of a mile from where we were camping to the switch track where the railroad cars were and I could hear the laughin' and talkin' and carryin' on that this invitation brought on and I knew long before Friole got back to camp that we were about to have a big Sunday.

Friole hung the goat up in a tree and butchered and dressed him before he went to bed so the meat would cool out during the night. Next morning all the men came over to camp before we were finished with breakfast and drank two pots of coffee while they visited and told about their horse experiences.

They took the goat and carried it back to the railroad house cars and the Captain had a key to the railroad stock pens which were nearby. He unlocked them and we gathered up all the horses and drove them into the stock pens. Stock pens in East Texas towns were not nearly as large as those in the West and this set of stock pens had one big corral and two small corrals that joined the loading shute.

These misplaced railroad cowboys were already having a lot of fun by hurrahin' each other about who could ride certain horses. Me and Choc caught and drove the gentle horses and work mules into one of the small corrals. We had brought the extra saddles over and plenty of rope and halters and me and Choc worked horseback putting two or three head of unbroke horses into the other small corral. Then these railroad cowboys would catch a horse and do whatever they had to to get a saddle on him and one of them would ride this horse around in this small corral where he wouldn't have room to buck for a little while and then I would open the gate to the big corral and this bronc would buck and run into the main herd of horses. There was lots of buckin' and laughin' and horse-breakin' went on all morning.

The women folks had took over doing the barbecue and

they were trying to outdo each other with garlic and pepper and the other kinds of stuff that they knew to use that would ruin most meat but would improve goat. By dinnertime, there was a few clothes tore and a little hide knocked off of the railroad cowboys but the horse workin' had improved appetites.

We had liver and fresh fried goat meat for dinner and the best parts that were being barbecued wouldn't be ready till supper. I ate as much meat and pepper and garlic as the rest of them. We went back to the stock pens after dinner and leaned back against the pens in the shade of trees and siesta'd and visited until that goat liver quit movin' around. Then we went back to breakin' horses.

By middle of the morning, I had begun to see that I was goin' to get a whole lot of good done on the forty-one unbroke horses that me and Choc had been having trouble building up nerve enough to ride. What was left unbroke were the older and rougher-actin' horses that were left out of the one hundred or so head that we started out with that never had been broke. The common wear and tear of drivin' and halterin' and handlin' had gentled these horses a lot but I thought I would make it interesting to these railroad cow-boys and told them that I was gonna pay them a dollar a head for all the horses that they rode until they stopped buckin'. Well, I think this made the horse breakin' a lot faster, and two of the six that weren't much stock hands had really begun to take hold.

Me and Choc did the horse work during the day, such as ropin' and snubbin' the broncs to saddle horns, and we led the worst ones around the big corral to keep them from buckin' so much. After all, I was tryin' to get these horses broke enough to sell to buyers and wasn't too interested in seeing how high they could throw these misplaced cowboys. By late afternoon I had a well-sapped-out, near-broke bunch of horses, and the railroad had a section crew that might be a little sore and stiff for Monday's work.

We gathered under the trees close to the railroad house cars. By now the women had sure fixed a big barbecue with beans and taters and pepper and all the rest of the Latin American trimmings and everybody had a big time. I think that extra money kept the skinned places and bruises from hurting too much. After supper we turned the horses out where they could graze and fill up from the day's horse workin'.

There had been a good many natives gathered during the day and set on the fence and watched the show. When bronc horses were being ridden and handled around a crowd of East Texas natives, it didn't generate any horse tradin' business because it was plain to see that they were a little rough for cotton pickers and cane growers. This made me think that the best thing to do the next day was to drift on deeper into the woods.

We camped the next night close to Waskom. Friole found some good farm people along the way and got them to sell him butter and eggs and chickens, and that night at supper we got most of that garlic out of our mouths from the night before.

For the next two or three days we sold gentle horses that we had traded for and those that were well broke including the feed man's mares, and the afternoon that we drove into a mule barn at Bossier City, Louisiana, we had forty-five head of horses and one pair of work mules.

By now my horse Concho had gotten to be a steady mount and had made a real good horse. I thought that we were far enough from home and it was early enough in the fall that there was some money in the country, and I had begun to think that I would like to sell out. Friole and Choc had begun to hurrah me about how was I goin' to give up Concho. I had been tellin' them for two or three days that he would be the last horse I would sell.

The mule barn at Bossier City had some big lots around it with shade trees and we were brushin' and curryin' and workin' on all our horses and tryin' to have some business when I had the bright idea that a big auction would be the way to sell plumb out of business.

I rode up to the printing office and asked about having some circulars printed to advertise a horse auction. The old printer helped me write out what would go on the circular and told me that he would print 500 for $2.50. I thought that would be a big bargain and he evidently had the time and needed the business because he printed them that afternoon and we were advertisin' a horse sale for Saturday at two o'clock. This gave us a few more days to get our horses ready.

Me and Choc rode around and scattered the circulars. I put them in all the stores and tacked them on telephone posts, and the next morning the mule barn was swarming with farmers and traders wanting to buy horses before the auction. I thought it would be smart to not sell any more horses and make them come to the auction. We took a lot of time to halter and lead and show horses but we refused to sell a horse until Saturday afternoon.

By sale time Saturday the fences were pretty well covered up with Cajun farmers ready to bid on these horses. We had spent that morning putting halters or lead ropes on all the horses and we had them tied around the fences and to the trees. I got up on a big stump in the middle of one of the corrals that was going to be my auction stand. I made a short speech about how good these horses were and how bad I wanted to sell 'em, and I stressed the fact that all these horses were all gentle to catch and lead and all of them had been rode and some them were broke to work. I didn't explain that they were all rode the Sunday afternoon before.

Choc led out the first horse; then Friole would lead with the next one. These Cajun farmers came off the fences and got down real close to look at the horses and look in their mouths and holler and ask questions.

Our bookkeeping system was real simple. When I got what I thought was the last bid on a horse and hollered "Sold," the buyer would come up to the stump and hand me his money and Choc or Friole would hand him the horse's halter rope. Then we would sell another horse.

About halfway through the horse sale, we rolled in the spring wagon and the harness and everything that we had that we weren't goin' to take back with us. I sold everything from the tin cups to the harness and collars at good enough prices. Then I started back in on the horses.

As these buyers got their horses, most of them took them back and retied 'em because they wanted to watch the rest of the sale and every time Friole or Choc led a horse around the stump, they would holler, while I was trying to get a bid, about how gentle the horse was and they would always wind up that he had been rode.

When the sale was over and all the horses were sold but Concho, some of these Cajuns were afoot and jumped on their new-bought horses bareback. Several led them off behind their wagons without much trouble, but two different men hooked their new-bought "teams" to their wagons and there was a good hour and a half of runaways and bronc ridin'. I didn't hear much whinin' or complainin' because the buyers were too busy tryin' to catch the horses that got away or too far off with the ones that had run away and the crowd got smaller until by late afternoon, we had our bedrolls and saddles we kept in the hall of the barn and I still had Concho.

During the day I had been waddin' money up and stickin' it in my pockets. I set down on my bedroll and straightened out my money and felt good about the whole trip. Since I had bought these horses cheap and drove 'em a long ways, this had been a successful trip. I paid Choc and Friole all I owed them and gave them an extra $20 apiece for travelin' money to get home on.

We went uptown that night and tried to eat up all the Creole grub there was in a Cajun café, went to the Saturday-night picture show, and walked back out to the barn. That was the only time I had been to town afoot since this drive started, but I would have felt a little ashamed to ride Concho along while Friole and Choc had to walk.

Next morning Friole wrapped all his belongin's up in that red bedspread that he had traded for and tied it together with a lariat rope. Choc had his bedroll tied with a lariat rope and both of them had cinched their saddles around their bedrolls just like you would cinch a saddle around a horse.

They hired a jitney to haul them and their riggin' across the river to Shreveport, where they was goin' to catch a train home. Choc was headed for Oklahoma and Friole was going to San Angelo, and when we shook hands and said good-bye, they was still hurrahin' me that I probably was goin' to ride Concho back home. I told them, no, that I would sell him at the depot platform in Shreveport just before I got on the train.

I tied all my riggin' on Concho and rode over to Shreveport about noon and I unsaddled Concho at the depot. A cowboy has all his belongin's in his pockets or wrapped up in his bedroll and when he is going to travel by train or bus, he would do his bedroll up real short and big around and then he would cinch his saddle over his bedroll and tie the saddle blanket and bridle to the saddle. This was considered the proper way for a cowboy to carry his luggage.

I went into the depot and bought a ticket to Greenville and I announced to the ticket agent and to the people in the waiting room that I was fixin' to sell a young grey horse at auction at the depot platform. I had had such good luck at my horse auction that I knew I could sell this good horse just before I got on the train.

I took Concho's lead rope and stood up on the depot platform and bellered a few times to where they could have heard me back to Bossier City, and all those people in the waiting room or in hearin' distance must have thought I was jokin' 'cause didn't nobody show up for the horse sale. The people in the waitin' room was just like me—they was fixin' to catch a train and didn't need to buy a horse! After I had made a speech about this horse that I thought would have been good enough to have sold a jackass, nobody bid. The station agent raised the window to his office and hollered, "I'll give $10."

About that time I heard the train whistle and hollered, "SOLD!"

A NOTE ABOUT THE AUTHOR

Ben K. Green, whose Horse Tradin' *and* Wild Cow Tales *and* The Village Horse Doctor: West of the Pecos *are already minor classics, at the very least, in a rich assemblage of Western Americana, was the kind of Westerner who almost crawled out of the cradle and into a saddle, spending his childhood, adolescence, and young manhood on horseback. He studied veterinary medicine in the United States and abroad and practiced in the Far Southwest in one of the last big horse countries in North America. When he eventually gave up his practice and research, he returned to his home town, Cumby, Texas, where until his death in 1974, he raised good horses and cattle.*

A NOTE ON THE TYPE

The text of this book was set on the Linotype in a new face called Primer, designed by Rudolph Ruzicka, earlier responsible for the design of Fairfield and Fairfield Medium, Linotype faces whose virtues have for some time now been accorded wide recognition.

The complete range of sizes of Primer was first made available in 1954, although the pilot size of 12 point was ready as early as 1951. The design of the face makes general reference to Linotype Century (long a serviceable type, totally lacking in manner or frills of any kind) but brilliantly corrects the characterless quality of that face.